JN362371

New+

GET UP TO SPEED

Situational

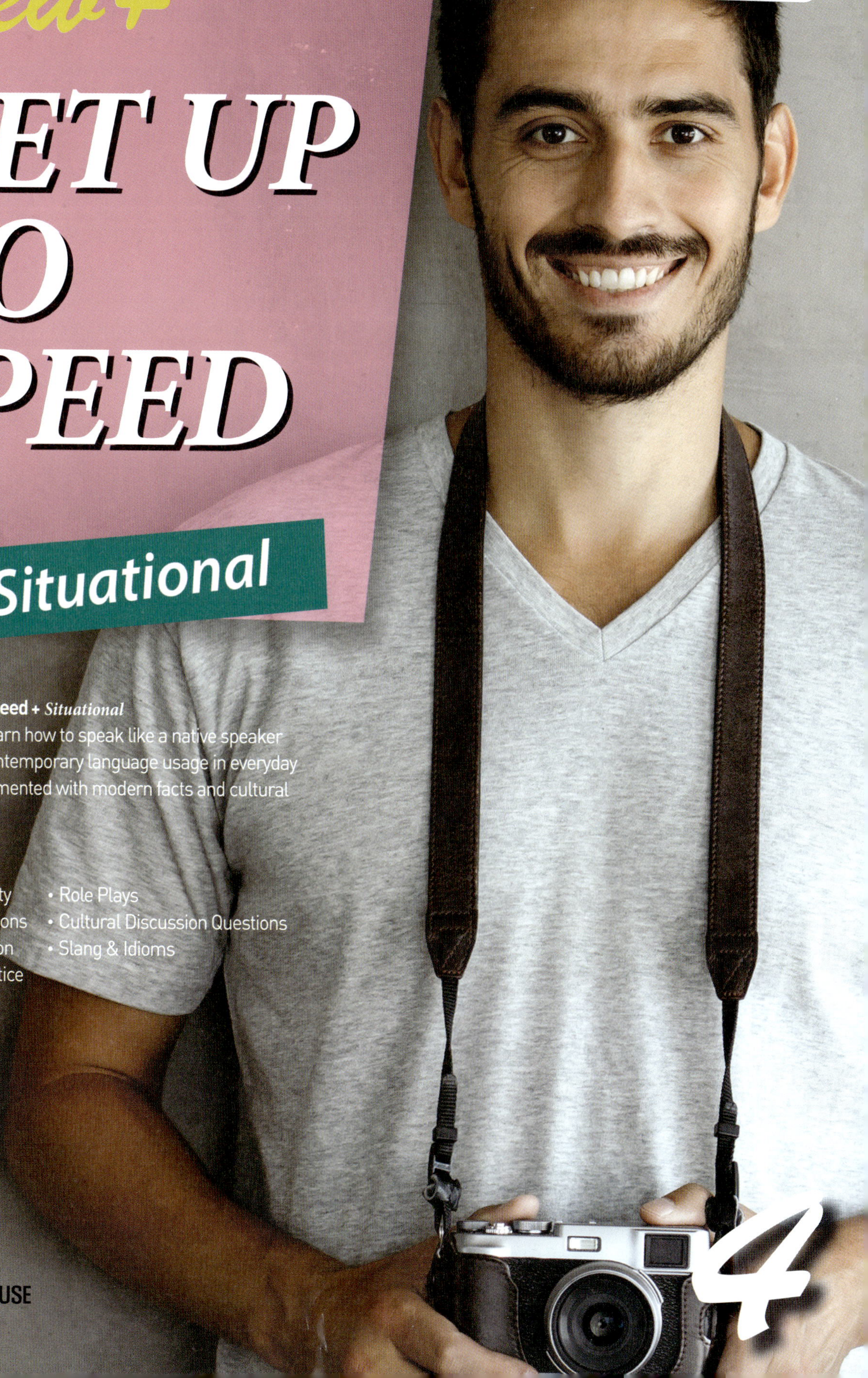

New Get Up to Speed + *Situational*
helps students learn how to speak like a native speaker by focusing on contemporary language usage in everyday situations supplemented with modern facts and cultural notions.

Key Features

- Warm Up Activity
- Useful Expressions
- Key Conversation
- Language Practice
- Role Plays
- Cultural Discussion Questions
- Slang & Idioms

4

MP3

CARROT HOUSE

CARROT HOUSE

New Get Up To Speed+ 4 Situational
© Carrot House

All rights reserved. No part of this publication may be reproduced,
stores in a retrieval system, or transmitted in any form or by any means
without the prior permission in writing of Carrot House.

Printed : First published January 2019
Reprinted September 2019

Author : Carrot Language Lab

ISBN 978-89-6732-294-6

Printed and distributed in Korea
9F, 488, Gangnam St. Gangnam-gu, Seoul, 06120, South Korea

Curriculum Map

Course	Level 1	Level 2	Level 3	Level 4	Level 5	Level 6	Level 7	Text Book
General Conversation	Essential English : Begin Again							
	Pre Get Up to Speed 1~2	New Get Up to Speed+ 1~2						
			New Get Up to Speed+ 3~4					
				New Get Up to Speed+ 5~6				
					New Get Up to Speed+ 7~8			
	Daily Focused English 1							
		Daily Focused English 2						
Discussion				Active Discussion 1				
					Active Discussion 2			
						Dynamic Discussion		
			Chicken Soup Course					
				Dynamic Information & Digital Technology				
Business Conversation	Pre Business Basics 1							
		Pre Business Basics 2						
			Business Basics 1					
				Business Basics 2				
					Business Practice 1			
						Business Practice 2		
Global Biz Workshop				Effective Business Writing Skills (Workbook)				
				Effective Presentation Skills (Workbook)				
					Effective Negotiation Skills (Workbook)			
					Cross-Cultural Training 1~2 (Workbook)			
					Leadership Training Course (Workbook)			
Business Skills				Simple & Clear Technical Writing Skills				
				Effective Business Writing Skills				
				Effective Meeting Skills				
				Business Communication (Negotiation)				
				Effective Presentation Skills				
					Marketing 1			
						Marketing 2		
						Management		
On the Job English				Human Resources				
				Accounting and Finance				
				Marketing and Sales				
				Production Management				
				Automotive				
				Banking and Commerce				
				Medical and Medicine				
				Information Technology				
				Construction				
			Construction English in Use 1 ~ 4					
			Public Service English in Use					

※ This Curriculum Map illustrates the entire line-up of textbooks at CARROT HOUSE.

CARROT HOUSE_2019.01

new+ GET UP TO SPEED
Situational

Introduction

Carrot House Methodology

Andragogical Approach & Productive English

The teaching of children (pedagogy) and adult learning (andragogy) are distinctively different. Pedagogy is akin to training and encourages convergent thinking and rote learning. It is compulsory, centered on the teacher and the imparting of information with minimal control by the learner. Andragogy, by contrast, is about education as freedom. It encourages divergent thinking and active learning. It is voluntary, learner oriented and opens up vistas for continual learning. Adults need to feel independent and in control of their learning. Therefore, Carrot House curriculum is based on andragogy and is designed to encourage learners' participation and engagement by providing more task-based activities and opportunities to frequently interact in the classroom. People want to achieve communicative competence when they learn other languages. English education in EFL environments has been rather focused on the receptive skills of English—listening and reading—which simply increases learners' knowledge about a language, not the competence of using it. If people are well equipped with productive skills—speaking and writing—they will be competent in English communication. This is why Carrot House curriculum is designed to enhance learners' productive skills throughout the course. This andragogical approach of the Carrot House Curriculum, which focuses on productive English, will enable learners to achieve communication skills necessary for global competence. Carrot House's teaching philosophy and curriculum combine to provide a "Language for Success" for all learners.

Communicative Language Learning (CLL)

This communicative interaction, the essential component of language acquisition, does not occur in a typical, non-meaningful, fun-oriented conversation with native speakers. It occurs in a negotiated interaction through which a well-trained teacher provides the comprehensible input that is appropriate to the learners. The learners, at the same time, actively utilize the opportunities given to them by the teachers. To this end, the Communicative Language Learning (CLL) method is employed in the field of Foreign Language Acquisition. The CLL method provides activities that are geared toward using language pragmatically, authentically and functionally with the intention of achieving meaningful purposes.

Course Overview

Features

Productive English
Learn to use practical and authentic expressions in various daily conversation, common collocations, written sentences, and activities.

Maximization of Schema
The use of visual texts, topic specific questions and useful expressions allow learners to find connections between the contents and their lives by maximizing their schema.

Interactive Activity
Activities, such as role-play, pair-work, group-work, and class-work, provide learners with the opportunity to constantly interact each other.

A Range of Everyday Topics
Through dealing with a range of daily situations in class, learners are equipped to tackle similar situations in reality.

Discussion
Learners can expand their ability to effectively express themselves in English through discussing a broad range of topics.

Slang / Idiom
Through learning topic-related slang and idioms, learners can improve their English language proficiency and use contemporary informal expressions to articulate their ideas.

Opinions on Topic-related Situations
Aims to enhance learner's abilities to speak logically. This task gives learners the chance to express their opinions on a given topic or from a choice of two situations.

Lesson Composition

Each New Get Up To Speed+ Situational book is composed of 12 lessons. Each lesson is composed of 7 main activities and 5 useful extra activities.

1. Warm Up Activity

To activate the students and their background knowledge, the lesson starts with discussing an image together with three situation-related-questions.

2. Useful Expression

Students can expand their English-language ability by practicing actively used expressions in various situations.

3. Key Conversation

Students can read, listen, and repeat how native speakers communicate with others on a daily basis. The activity also includes questions to test comprehension skills.

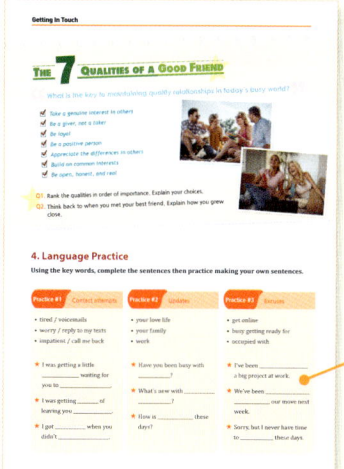

4. Language Practice

Students can practice using key words and expressions to complete sentences and create their own sentences. This helps students to apply and remember what they have learned.

Lesson Composition

Each New Get Up To Speed+ Situational book is composed of 12 lessons. Each lesson is composed of 7 main activities and 5 useful extra activities.

5. Role Plays

Task-based role plays puts off the burden of acting but focuses on the language and task achievement and ability to express oneself in various situations.

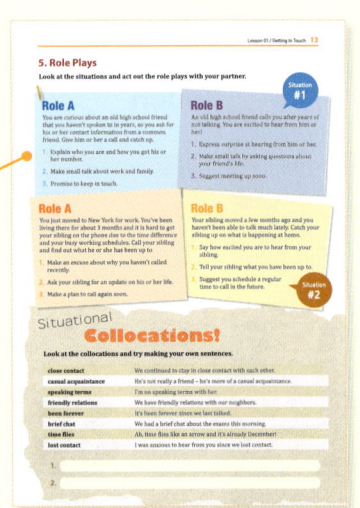

6. Cultural Discussion Questions

Gives the learners the opportunity to share, learn, and discuss global, cultural, and personal opinions and notions.

7. Slang & Idioms

Reinforce the learner's ability to speak English like a native through the use of situational contemporary slang & idioms.

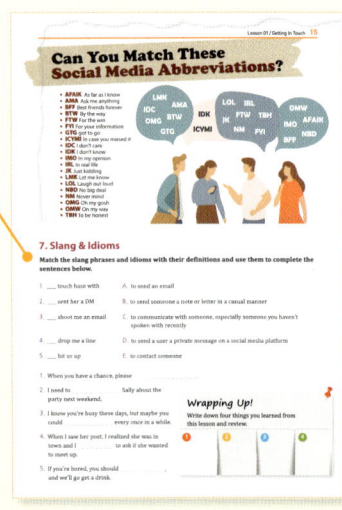

Extra Activities

Each lesson includes five extra activities: three engaging facts and figures, Situational Collocations, and Did You Know?. These activities provides students with both popular and intriguing global facts. These can also be used to help facilitate a more fun and enjoyable class.

Contents

Title	Learning Objective	Expression Check	
Lesson 1 Getting In Touch	To contact people whom you have not spoken with recently.	- Hey, John, long time no hear. - What's new and exciting with you? - What have you been up to these days?	10
Lesson 2 Paying the Bill	To treat your friends to a meal at a restaurant.	- How was everything? - Is this together or on separate checks? - Will this be cash or credit?	16
Lesson 3 Treat Yourself	To ask and respond to questions related to purchasing jewelry and other expensive goods.	- Could I take a look at that one? - I want to have the band engraved inside. - When did this design come out?	22
Lesson 4 Planning a Potluck	To plan a potluck dinner with friends.	- Would you mind bringing a salad? - How about bringing your homemade chili? - Let's see if Mary can bring a salad.	28
Lesson 5 Buying Tickets	To inquire about and buy tickets for different events.	- Do you have any tickets left for the concert? - How much are the tickets going for? - Which type of tickets do you want?	34
Lesson 6 Congratulations!	To offer congratulations on the birth of a child.	- He is as cute as a button. - He looks just like his father! - How are mother and baby doing?	40
Lesson 7 Volunteer Work	To describe and discuss volunteer experiences with others.	- I'd like to give back to the community. - I just want to make a difference. - Could you lend a hand here?	46
Lesson 8 TGIF	To express excitement about the weekend.	- I can't wait for this day to be over! - I'm counting down the minutes to the weekend. - I'm hoping to knock off early today.	52
Lesson 9 Grabbing a Drink	To make plans with colleagues after work.	- Are you up for drinks after work today? - You don't have to ask me twice. - I'm sure you can twist my arm.	58
Lesson 10 Borrowing Money	To go to a bank and apply for a personal loan.	- I'd like to apply for a personal loan. - Why do you need the loan? - What kind of rates can you offer me?	64
Lesson 11 The Post Office	To complete tasks at the post office.	- I have some letters to mail. - Do you want to send it standard post or airmail? - How long does airmail take?	70
Lesson 12 Picking Up a Prescription	To speak with a pharmacist about a prescription.	- I need this prescription filled, please. - When do you think I can pick it up? - Do you have health insurance?	76

Slang & Idioms — 82

Answer Key — 84

Getting In Touch

Getting In Touch

01

» Learning Objective

Upon completion of this lesson, you will be able to...

contact people whom you have not spoken with recently.

» Expression Check

☑ Hey, John, long time no hear.
☑ What's new with you?
☑ What have you been up to these days?

1. Warm Up Activity

Describe what is happening in the picture.

Talk about the questions.

1. Do you prefer to keep in touch with people using the phone, email, or social media?
2. Is it easy for you to keep up with your friends and family these days? Why or why not?
3. What is your least favorite form of communication? Why?

2. Useful Expressions

Match the expressions (a-d) to its similar meaning (1-4).

A What have you been up to lately?　★　　★ **1** You haven't posted on social media recently.

B Long time no hear!　★　　★ **2** How are things?

C What's up?　★　　★ **3** It's been forever!

D I haven't seen you pop up on my feed lately.　★　　★ **4** What's been going on in your life?

3. Key Conversation

🎧 Think of the useful expressions and practice the dialogue.

Long Time No Hear!

Rachael Hey, long time no hear! How's it going?

Tiffany Great! Sorry I didn't reply to your message. I saw the text a week ago, but I've been so busy that I forgot to reply.

Rachael No worries. I'm just glad to talk with you.

Tiffany I'm so happy you called. It's been way too long! So what have you been up to these days?

Rachael Just the same old, same old, you know. Hey! Did you hear that Ken is getting married in February?

Tiffany Are you serious? I thought they were going to have a big bash down here next summer.

Rachael No- don't you ever get on Facebook or Twitter?

Tiffany Not lately, I've been too busy with work to look at it.

Rachael Well, anyway, there's that, and I'm seeing someone new!

Tiffany I knew it. I don't talk to you for a month, and I'm completely out of the loop!

Questions

1. How do Rachael and Tiffany keep in touch?

2. Do you think Rachael and Tiffany are close friends? Why or why not?

3. What do you think Tiffany has been up to lately?

4. Does it usually take you a long time to get in touch with your friends or family?

Getting In Touch

THE 7 QUALITIES OF A GOOD FRIEND

"What is the key to maintaining quality relationships in today's busy world?"

- ☑ Take a genuine interest in others
- ☑ Be a giver, not a taker
- ☑ Be loyal
- ☑ Be a positive person
- ☑ Appreciate the differences in others
- ☑ Build on common interests
- ☑ Be open, honest, and real

Q1. Rank the qualities in order of importance. Explain your choices.

Q2. Think back to when you met your best friend. Explain how you grew close.

4. Language Practice

Using the key words, complete the sentences then practice making your own sentences.

Practice #1 Contact attempts

- tired / voicemails
- worry / reply to my texts
- impatient / call me back

★ I was getting a little _____ waiting for you to _____.

★ I was getting _____ of leaving you _____.

★ I got _____ when you didn't _____.

Practice #2 Updates

- your love life
- your family
- work

★ Have you been busy with _____?

★ What's new with _____?

★ How is _____ these days?

Practice #3 Excuses

- get online
- busy getting ready for
- occupied with

★ I've been _____ a big project at work.

★ We've been _____ _____ our move next week.

★ Sorry, but I never have time to _____ these days.

5. Role Plays

Look at the situations and act out the role plays with your partner.

Situation #1

Role A
You are curious about an old high school friend that you haven't spoken to in years, so you ask for his or her contact information from a common friend. Give him or her a call and catch up.

1. Explain who you are and how you got his or her number.
2. Make small talk about work and family.
3. Promise to keep in touch.

Role B
An old high school friend calls you after years of not talking. You are excited to hear from him or her!

1. Express surprise at hearing from him or her.
2. Make small talk by asking questions about your friend's life.
3. Suggest meeting up soon.

Situation #2

Role A
You just moved to New York for work. You've been living there for about 3 months and it is hard to get your sibling on the phone due to the time difference and your busy working schedules. Call your sibling and find out what he or she has been up to.

1. Make an excuse about why you haven't called recently.
2. Ask your sibling for an update on his or her life.
3. Make a plan to call again soon.

Role B
Your sibling moved a few months ago and you haven't been able to talk much lately. Catch up with your sibling on what is happening at home.

1. Say how excited you are to hear from your sibling.
2. Tell your sibling what you have been up to.
3. Suggest you schedule a regular time to call in the future.

Situational Collocations!

Look at the collocations and try making your own sentences.

close contact	We continued to stay in close contact with each other.
casual acquaintance	He's not really a friend – he's more of a casual acquaintance.
speaking terms	I'm on speaking terms with her.
friendly relations	We have friendly relations with our neighbors.
been forever	It's been forever since we last talked.
brief chat	We had a brief chat about the exams this morning.
time flies	Ah, time flies like an arrow and it's already December!
lost contact	I was anxious to hear from you since we lost contact.

1.
2.

Getting In Touch

Top 3 Ways to Stay in Touch with Friends

01 twitter — Twitter is the new gold standard for lightning-fast communication.

02 skype — Skype is an affordable and easy way to call friends living around the globe.

03 facebook — Facebook has become a popular way of communicating and sharing photos and other information with friends and family.

Q. What method do you usually use to keep in touch with your friends or family?

6. Cultural Discussion Questions

Talk about the questions in as much detail as possible.

1. How do you think that social networking sites have changed the way you communicate with your friends?

2. When you talk to a friend for the first time in a while, what is usually your first question? Why?

3. Do you think it is important to communicate with your friends often in order to maintain good relationships? Why or why not?

4. In your country, what is the most common way for people your age to keep in touch?

Did You Know?

Read and discuss how you feel about each fact.

1. Did you know that approximately *1.28 billion people* are active on *Facebook every month*? That's a number roughly equivalent to the entire population of India.

2. Did you know that American *adults under 45* send and receive an average of more than *85 texts a day*?

Can You Match These Social Media Abbreviations?

- **AFAIK** As far as I know
- **AMA** Ask me anything
- **BFF** Best friends forever
- **BTW** By the way
- **FTW** For the win
- **FYI** For your information
- **GTG** got to go
- **ICYMI** In case you missed it
- **IDC** I don't care
- **IDK** I don't know
- **IMO** In my opinion
- **IRL** In real life
- **JK** Just kidding
- **LMK** Let me know
- **LOL** Laugh out loud
- **NBD** No big deal
- **NM** Never mind
- **OMG** Oh my gosh
- **OMW** On my way
- **TBH** To be honest

7. Slang & Idioms

Match the slang phrases and idioms with their definitions and use them to complete the sentences below.

1. ___ touch base with   A. to send an email
2. ___ sent her a DM   B. to send someone a note or letter in a casual manner
3. ___ shoot me an email   C. to communicate with someone, especially someone you haven't spoken with recently
4. ___ drop me a line   D. to send a user a private message on a social media platform
5. ___ hit us up   E. to contact someone

1. When you have a chance, please _____.
2. I need to _____ Sally about the party next weekend.
3. I know you're busy these days, but maybe you could _____ every once in a while.
4. When I saw her post, I realized she was in town and I _____ to ask if she wanted to meet up.
5. If you're bored, you should _____, and we'll go get a drink.

Wrapping Up!
Write down four things you learned from this lesson and review.

1.
2.
3.
4.

02 Paying the **Bill**

» **Learning Objective**

Upon completion of this lesson, you will be able to…

treat your friends to a meal at a restaurant.

» **Expression Check**

- ☑ How was everything?
- ☑ Is this together or on separate checks?
- ☑ Will this be cash or credit?

1. Warm Up Activity

Describe what is happening in the picture.

Talk about the questions.

1. Do you often treat your friends to a meal?
2. What is the most common way to pay for a meal in your country?
3. When was the last time you ate out with a friend? How did you pay?

2. Useful Expressions

Match the expressions (a-d) to its similar meaning (1-4).

- A Is this on separate checks?
- B How would you like to pay?
- C Could you bring me the check, please?
- D How was everything this evening?

- 1 Did you enjoy your meal?
- 2 Bring me the bill, please.
- 3 Would you like a separate bill for each person?
- 4 Are you paying by cash or credit card?

3. Key Conversation

Think of the useful expressions and practice the dialogue.

Check, Please

George: I'm stuffed. I can't eat another bite. Should we just get the check and go?

Waiter: How was everything tonight, sir? Can I bring you anything else?

George: Everything was just great, thanks.

Waiter: Would either of you like tea or coffee?

George: Not for me, thank you. Could we just get the check, please?

Waiter: One moment, sir... Here you are. I can take care of that for you whenever you're ready.

George: We're ready now. I'll put it on my credit card.

Waiter: Thank you, sir. I'll be right back with your bill to sign.

George: Thank you.

Questions

1. Do you think George enjoyed his meal?
2. Do you think this restaurant has good service?
3. Why didn't George want anything else?
4. What do you think will happen next?

Paying the Bill

Tipping Guidelines

(1) Dining
★ **Server at a full-service restaurant:** 15% to 20% of the total bill
★ **Sommelier:** 15% to 20% of the total wine expenditures
★ **Delivery person:** 5% to 10% of the total bill

(2) At the Bar
★ **Bartender:** 10% to 15% of the total drink bill
★ If the bar is particularly crowded, be certain to tip generously after each round.
★ If the bartender sends any complimentary drinks your way, tip about half the value of that round.

Q. What are some other situations when you might be expected to tip?

4. Language Practice
Using the key words, complete the sentences then practice making your own sentences.

Practice #1 — Setting a bill
- the check
- the bill
- a receipt

★ Would you mind bringing me _____?

★ Could we get _____ for this?

★ Could I have _____, please?

Practice #2 — Payment method
- credit card
- cash
- a gift certificate

★ I want to settle up with _____.

★ I'll be paying with _____.

★ I'm going to put this on my _____.

Practice #3 — Finishing dinner
- bring the bill
- just the check
- settle up

★ No, thank you. Just _____ _____, please.

★ Not tonight. I'd like to _____ _____ when you get a moment.

★ Nothing else for me. _____.

5. Role Plays

Look at the situations and act out the role plays with your partner.

Situation #1

Role A
You are a customer who would like to pay the dinner bill for you and your friend.

1. Decline ordering anything else.
2. Ask to pay together on one check.
3. Say you will pay by credit card.

Role B
You are a server who must help a customer take care of his or her bill.

1. Ask if the customers would like coffee or dessert.
2. Offer to bring separate checks.
3. Ask how the customer will be paying.

Situation #2

Role A
You are dining out for your father's birthday. Your father never lets you pay for anything, but you really want to treat him to dinner. Talk to the server and arrange to pay secretly while your father is in the bathroom.

1. Explain why you want to pay in advance.
2. Say you will pay by credit card.
3. Thank the server for his or her help.

Role B
You are a server at a restaurant. Help the customer pay for a meal.

1. Agree to help the customer.
2. Ask to take the customer's credit card now to help him or her pay secretly.
3. Offer to bring some complimentary dessert to celebrate the customer's father's birthday.

Situational Collocations!

Look at the collocations and try making your own sentences.

all on me	Choose anything you want, it's all on me.
my treat	This is my treat.
I insist	You paid last time. I Insist. It's on me.
have receipt	Could I have a receipt for that please?
handle the bill	Guys, let me handle the bill.
generous tip	Mike gave a generous tip for the good service.
tax included	The check came to fifty dollars, tax included.
figure out	Could you figure out how much it costs in total?

1. ....
2. ....

Paying the Bill

Cash vs. Credit Card

Credit cards are a tool that users can use to access a line of credit from a bank or other lender. They allow people to pay for things that they may not have the cash to pay for at the moment. In addition, credit cards often offer users special benefits, such as discounts and airline miles.

Q1. How many credit cards do you have?

Q2. Do you prefer to pay with cash or by credit card? Why?

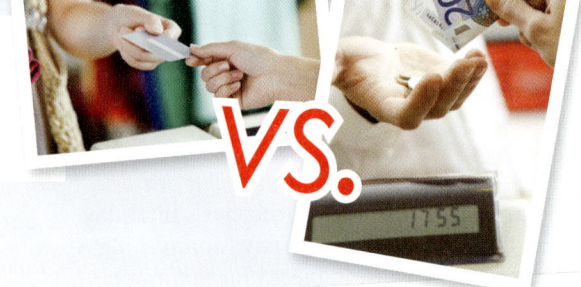

6. Cultural Discussion Questions

Talk about the questions in as much detail as possible.

1. How much money do you usually spend on eating out each month?
2. Is it common to tip waiters and waitresses in your country? If so, how much is expected?
3. What do you think about restaurants automatically adding a tip onto a customer's bill?
4. Describe the best meal you have ever enjoyed at a restaurant. How much did you pay? What made the experience so enjoyable?

Did You Know?

Read and discuss how you feel about each fact.

1. Did you know that the credit card companies charge businesses **5%** for every customer transaction?
2. Did you know that the average tip these days at a restaurant is **15%** of the total bill?

Which Word?

When we talk about payments, we use many different words to describe different kinds of costs. Discuss the differences between the following words.

When you pay for a service, which words do you use?

When you pay for travel and transportation, which words do you use?

7. Slang & Idioms

Match the slang phrases and idioms with their definitions and use them to complete the sentences below.

1. ___ hard cash
2. ___ strapped
3. ___ money to burn
4. ___ service charge
5. ___ charged it

A. to pay with a credit card
B. to have a lot of money to spend on things that are unnecessary
C. to be short of money
D. money in the form of coins or notes
E. an extra charge added for a service

1. Could you cover this? I'm a little _____ until payday.
2. There's a _____ on the check. Does that mean I don't need to tip?
3. I didn't have enough cash on me to pay for the check, so I _____.
4. I've got this! I have some _____.
5. They don't accept credit cards there. We will need to bring _____.

Wrapping Up!

Write down four things you learned from this lesson and review.

1. _____
2. _____
3. _____
4. _____

Treat Yourself

03 Treat **Yourself**

» **Learning Objective**

Upon completion of this lesson, you will be able to...
ask and respond to questions related to purchasing jewelry and other expensive goods.

» **Expression Check**

- ☑ Could I take a look at that one?
- ☑ I want to have the band engraved inside.
- ☑ When did this design come out?

1. Warm Up Activity

Describe what is happening in the picture.

Talk about the questions.

1. What is the most expensive item that you have ever purchased for yourself?
2. What are some occasions when people might want to treat themselves or others to expensive items?
3. What is your favorite place to shop when you want to treat yourself to something nice? Why?

2. Useful Expressions

Match the expressions (a-d) to its similar meaning (1-4).

A. When did this watch come out?

B. I want to have the band engraved inside.

C. What kind of cut are you looking for?

D. The product comes with a lifetime guarantee.

1. I'd like a special message written on the ring.

2. What year was this design first made?

3. What shape would you like the stone to be?

4. The company will repair the item if something happens.

3. Key Conversation

Think of the useful expressions and practice the dialogue.

A Graduation Present

Sales Clerk: Can I help you find something special today?

Mattie: Yes, we're looking for a watch to get our son for a graduation present.

Sales Clerk: Well we have many styles to choose from. Have you decided on a particular style yet?

Mattie: We'd like something classic with a leather band. We want one that he will be able to wear for the rest of his life.

Sales Clerk: What type of face do you have in mind?

Mattie: I think we want to go for something round, but we are open to seeing other styles.

Sales Clerk: Take a look at these. We have a variety of classic watches that I think would be perfect for your son.

Mattie: It's so hard to choose. Which one is your most popular?

Sales Clerk: Why don't you take a look at this one?

Mattie: It's just gorgeous! Can I see this one here as well? It's such a hard decision!

Questions

1. Do you think Mattie will buy a watch today? Why or why not?
2. Do you think her son should be part of the decision?
3. Do you think a watch is a good graduation present? Explain.
4. Do you think a jeweler is the best place to make this purchase?

Treat Yourself

Splurge Worthy

People tend to splurge and buy unnecessary items which they regret later. However, there are some expensive purchases that are worth the investment. Below are the top 10 people say is a worthy splurge.

- Bed / Mattress
- Personal Dental Care
- Grocery Food
- Personal Trainer
- Home Theater System
- Work Clothes & Shoes
- Real Estate
- College Education
- Vacation
- Insurance & Safety

Q1. Why do you think these items are worth the splurge?

Q2. What are some of your personal expensive splurges? Was it worth it? Why?

4. Language Practice

Using the key words, complete the sentences then practice making your own sentences.

Practice #1 — Talking about details

- platinum
- total carat weight
- engraved

★ Could I have this _____?

★ What is the _____ _____ of the diamonds?

★ Does this band come in _____?

Practice #2 — Setting a budget

- $1,000 to $2,000
- under $1,000
- up to $500

★ I want the best ring I can get for _____.

★ I'm looking for something in the _____ range.

★ I'd be willing to go _____ for the right style.

Practice #3 — Guarantees

- certificate of authenticity
- good exchange policy
- warranty

★ Don't worry. This store offers a _____ _____ if you change your mind.

★ Be sure to save your _____ _____ in case you need to get it repaired later.

★ Minor damage is covered under the _____.

5. Role Plays

Look at the situations and act out the role plays with your partner.

Situation #1

Role A

You just got a big promotion at work! Visit a department store and treat yourself to a new work bag as a reward. You will need to carry your laptop in it as well as other documents.

1. Explain what you are looking for.
2. Tell what material you would like.
3. Describe what you will be carrying in the bag.

Role B

Help a customer decide on a new work bag. Ask questions about his or her specific needs to make a good recommendation.

1. Ask what material the customer is interested in.
2. Ask what items the customer will be carrying.
3. Ask about the customer's preferred style.

Situation #2

Role A

It's your mother's birthday. You want to give her a nice ring to show her what she means to you. She usually wears white gold and prefers simple, classic styles.

1. Tell the clerk who you are shopping for.
2. Explain what you want to buy.
3. Describe your mother's basic style.

Role B

You are a salesperson at a jewelry store. A customer comes in looking for a birthday present for his or her mother.

1. Ask what item the customer is looking for.
2. Ask about the style of the gift recipient.
3. Suggest a few designs for the customer to look at.

Situational Collocations!

Look at the collocations and try making your own sentences.

gift wrap	Could you gift wrap this please?
pay day	I always buy myself something nice on pay day.
wish list	I mark things I want to buy on a wish list.
on sale	I'm waiting for the golf club sets to go on sale.
reward myself	After a big project, I always reward myself to a fancy dinner.
give a discount	Could you give me a discount?
under warranty	It's still under warranty, so we'll fix it free of charge.
exclusive offer	This exclusive offer is available by using this link only.

1.
2.

Treat Yourself

Black Friday and Cyber Monday are famous shopping season that come right after Thanksgiving, an American holiday in November. It also signs the start of the Christmas shopping season. Although it originated in the U.S., it is now marketed in many countries around the world.

BLACK FRIDAY VS CYBER MONDAY

Black Friday
Day after Thanksgiving
Retail Stores

- Technology
- Small appliances
- Kitchenware
- Apple products

Cyber Monday
First Tuesday after Black Friday
Online Stores

- Clothing & Fashion
- Shoes
- Toys
- Beauty products

Q1. Is Black Friday or Cyber Monday marketed in your country? If so, do you take advantage of it?
Q2. Would you usually wait to buy something when it's on sale? Why?

6. Cultural Discussion Questions

Talk about the questions in as much detail as possible.

1. What are the most popular luxury goods that people in your country buy?
2. If someone gave you $10,000 to spend on one item for yourself, what would you buy?
3. Tell about an item that you saved up to buy. What was it? How did you choose it?
4. Are there any expensive items that people typically give for gifts in your country?

Did You Know?

Read and discuss how you feel about each fact.

1. Did you know that the average price of a *diamond engagement ring* in the US is *$6,163*?
2. Did you know that the top three *graduation gifts for men* are a nice *watch*, a new *laptop*, and a *professional wardrobe*?

7. Slang & Idioms

Match the slang phrases and idioms with their definitions and use them to complete the sentences below.

1. ___ splurge
2. ___ declare your purchase
3. ___ feel like a million bucks
4. ___ making money hand over fist
5. ___ burning a hole in my pocket

A. money that one wishes to spend quickly (often on something frivolous)
B. something that cost more money than one might ordinarily spend
C. to earn money fast and in large amounts
D. to feel wonderful
E. to formally list items purchased abroad on a customs form

1. I thought I would treat myself since I have that bonus money _____.
2. I _____ in my new suit!
3. My new bag was definitely a _____, but I know I'm going to use it for years.
4. Since my sister started that new job, she is _____.
5. Don't forget to _____ when you return home or you could be hit with a fine.

Wrapping Up!
Write down four things you learned from this lesson and review.

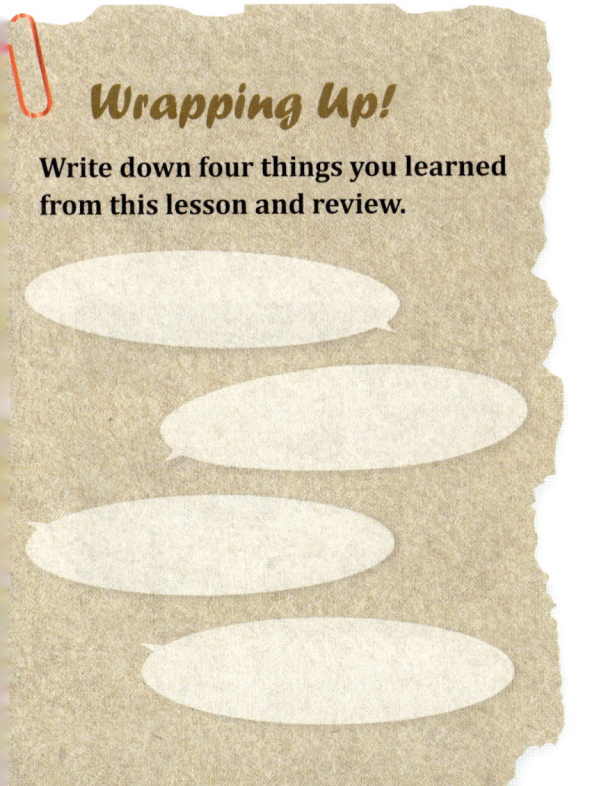

Birthstones

Different gemstones are not only valuable, but they are also traditionally associated with different personality traits. Each month has its own unique birthstone, which is said to represent certain characteristics of people born in that month. Look at the chart below to find what gem represents your birth month.

Month	Birthstone	Symbol
January	garnet	constancy, faith, and truth
February	amethyst	sincerity, sobriety, tranquility, protection, and peace
March	aquamarine	courage
April	diamond	innocence, purity, love, eternity, and strength
May	emerald	new life, love, and success
June	pearl	health, prosperity, long life, chastity, and modesty
July	ruby	contentment, harmony, and protection
August	peridot	courage and family happiness
September	sapphire	faith, purity, and clear thinking
October	opal	purity, innocence, and hope
November	topaz	sanity, healing, friendship, and fidelity
December	turquoise	fortune, luck, prosperity, and contentment

Q1. Which month were you born in? What is your birthstone?

Q2. Do you think the symbols are well-matched to your characteristics?

Planning a Potluck

04 Planning a Potluck

» Learning Objective

Upon completion of this lesson, you will be able to...

plan a potluck dinner with friends.

» Expression Check

- ☑ Would you mind bringing a salad?
- ☑ How about bringing your homemade chili?
- ☑ Let's see if Mary can bring a salad.

1. Warm Up Activity

Describe what is happening in the picture.

Talk about the questions.

1. Have you ever been to a potluck before?
2. Do you feel comfortable eating food made by someone else?
3. Do you think it is easier to prepare something hot or cold for a potluck dinner?

Lesson 04 / Planning a Potluck

2. Useful Expressions

Match the expressions (a-d) to its similar meaning (1-4).

A. We have enough food to feed an army.

B. Would you mind bringing your Southern fried chicken?

C. My eyes are bigger than my stomach at potlucks.

D. We have a real assortment of food here.

1. I usually eat too much food at potluck dinners.

2. There are so many different kinds of food to try.

3. We have so much food to eat.

4. Could you bring some of your famous fried chicken?

3. Key Conversation

Think of the useful expressions and practice the dialogue.

Organizing a Potluck

Lucy	So Carol, we have about 30 people coming to the annual summer potluck on Saturday, so we need to organize the food.
Carol	That shouldn't be difficult since most of our friends are great cooks.
Lucy	Would you mind bringing your homemade chili? I hear it's really good.
Carol	Sure, not a problem. I'll make up a double batch.
Lucy	How about we ask Mary to bring her Southern fried chicken? I've had it before, and I'm sure everyone will love it.
Carol	Let's ask Wendy to bring her Caesar salad.
Lucy	I wonder if Karen could bring her chocolate cream pie.
Carol	I'm sure she will. I just know my eyes will be bigger than my stomach at this potluck.
Lucy	I'm sure we'll have enough food to feed an army.
Carol	I can't wait until Saturday so I can sink my teeth into all of this delicious food.
Lucy	I know! It's going to be so good.

Questions

1. Do you think Lucy and Carol have planned the food well?
2. Do you think the people at the potluck will enjoy the food?
3. Which food would you like to try at their potluck?
4. What would you bring if you were going to their potluck?

Planning a Potluck

Tips for a Potluck Party

✓ Easy to Transport
Dishes should be easy to transport and need no more preparation at the party than perhaps reheating.

01

✓ Disposable Container
Remind guests to bring their dish in a disposable container. If this is not possible, ask them to mark the dish somehow so that you can get it back to them.

02

✓ Easy to Eat
Since potlucks usually include a large amount of people, not everyone will have a place to sit at a table. If this is the case with your potluck, make sure that you suggest that guests bring foods that do not have to be cut with a knife or that are easy to eat with one hand.

03

✓ Food Allergies
Be mindful of guests who may have allergies. Be sure to ask about food allergies and ask guests to put a list of ingredients on their dishes.

04

4. Language Practice

Using the key words, complete the sentences then practice making your own sentences.

Practice #1 — Checking on food

- short on
- hot dish
- bring salad

★ Do you think we have enough _____?

★ We might be _____ desserts.

★ I think we might have too many people _____.

Practice #2 — Asking for contributions

- pasta salad
- something sweet
- the paper plates

★ Would you mind bringing _____?

★ How about you bring _____?

★ Could you bring that _____ you make?

Practice #3 — Organizing a potluck

- people / coming to
- planning on / the potluck
- food / to bring

★ When are you _____ _____ having _____?

★ What kind of _____ do you want people _____?

★ How many _____ are _____ the potluck?

5. Role Plays

Look at the situations and act out the role plays with your partner.

Situation #1

Role A

Your family is hosting a family reunion potluck. You are short on desserts. Call your cousin and ask if he or she can bring one of his or her famous cheesecakes.

1. Explain why you are calling.
2. Thank your cousin.
3. Say that you have enough of everything else.

Role B

Your cousin calls to ask you to bring something to a family reunion potluck.

1. Say that you would be happy to make it.
2. Ask if you need to bring anything else.
3. Thank your cousin for planning the potluck.

Situation #2

Role A

You and your old friends are trying to arrange a potluck picnic in the park. Talk to your friend about what kind of things you need to plan.

1. Ask what foods are best for a picnic.
2. Discuss whether you should bring drinks or buy them at the park.
3. Discuss what equipment and other things need to be brought.

Role B

You and your old friends are trying to arrange a potluck picnic in the park. Talk to your friend about what kind of things you need to prepare.

1. Suggest some foods that your group can bring.
2. Give your opinion on what drinks you need.
3. Offer to bring picnic blankets.

Situational Collocations!

Look at the collocations and try making your own sentences.

fix a date	Let me know when you're free, and we'll fix a date for the meeting.
come by	You should come by this Friday, were having a potluck!
favorite dish	I'm going to prepare my favorite dish, spring rolls with fish sauce.
throw a party	She decided to throw a party and invite all her customers.
plastic utensils	I'll prepare the plastic utensils along with the outdoor tables.
finger food	No need to prepare any utensils, everything will be finger food.
festive mood	The entire country was caught up in a festive mood.
bottoms up	Happy New Year, cheers and bottoms up!

1. ....

2. ....

Planning a Potluck

6. Cultural Discussion Questions

Talk about the questions in as much detail as possible.

1. What kinds of food would people from your country bring if they were invited to a potluck?
2. Are potluck meals a good way to try out new recipes?
3. What occasions would be a good time to plan a potluck meal?
4. What dish are you most confident making? Would it be good to bring to a potluck?

Did You Know?

Read and discuss how you feel about each fact.

1. Did you know that *brownies* are one of the *most popular desserts* to bring to a potluck?
2. Did you know that having a potluck meal is *a great way to bring people together at a low cost*?

Get Together!

Match the following party descriptions to their names.

- (HOUSEWARMING PARTY)
- (BABY SHOWER)
- (PAJAMA PARTY)
- (POTLUCK)

★ A party most commonly held by children or teenagers, where a guest or guests are invited to stay overnight at the home of a friend, sometimes to celebrate birthdays or other special events

★ A party held within approximately 90 days of moving into a new residence, which is an occasion for the hosts to present their new home to their friends and for friends to give gifts to furnish the new home

★ A gathering of people where each person or group of people contributes a dish of food prepared by the person or the group of people to be shared among the group

★ A party to celebrate the pending or recent birth of a child by presenting gifts to the parents

7. Slang & Idioms

Match the slang phrases and idioms with their definitions and use them to complete the sentences below.

1. ___ leftovers
2. ___ go back for seconds
3. ___ piece of cake
4. ___ help yourself
5. ___ chow down

A. to eat food quickly or in an enthusiastic way
B. something easily achieved
C. to take some of what you want
D. food that remains after some has been consumed
E. to take a second helping of food

1. Don't be afraid to _____. There's plenty to go around.

2. Organizing a potluck dinner is a _____.

3. Just _____. The plates are over there.

4. The only problem with a potluck meal is we always have so many _____.

5. I can't wait to _____ at this potluck dinner.

Wrapping Up!

Write down four things you learned from this lesson and review.

1. _____
2. _____
3. _____
4. _____

05 Buying Tickets

» Learning Objective

Upon completion of this lesson, you will be able to...

inquire about and buy tickets for different events.

» Expression Check

- ☑ Do you have any tickets left for the concert?
- ☑ How much are the tickets going for?
- ☑ Which type of tickets do you want?

1. Warm Up Activity

Describe what is happening in the picture.

Talk about the questions.

1. What kinds of concerts and events are held in your city?
2. What is the most memorable event that you have ever bought a ticket for?
3. What is one upcoming event or show you would like to attend, and why?

Lesson 05 / Buying Tickets

2. Useful Expressions

Match the expressions (a-d) to its similar meaning (1-4).

A. The line starts over there.

B. How much are the tickets going for?

C. General admission seats are cheaper than orchestra ones.

D. I want to get my tickets before they are sold out.

1. The main seating is less expensive than the seats up front.

2. How much do the tickets cost?

3. The line begins on the other side.

4. I'd like to get my tickets as soon as possible.

3. Key Conversation

Think of the useful expressions and practice the dialogue.

A Don't-Miss Show

Cashier Next in line, please. How may I help you today, sir?

Josh Hi, do you have any tickets left for the concert?

Cashier Yes, we do. How many would you like to purchase?

Josh It'll just be me and my wife. How much are they going for?

Cashier With the service charge, it comes to $39.95 per ticket.

Josh OK, that's not so bad. We'll take two, then.

Cashier We have two on the end, Row L, in orchestra. We also have two in the middle, but closer up, in Row E.

Josh Let's have the ones on the end, please. Here's my credit card.

Cashier That'll be $79.90. Sign here and here are your tickets.

Josh Thanks. Oh, and what time do the doors open?

Cashier The lobby opens at 6:00 and the show starts at 7:00. Enjoy the show!

Josh Thanks! I'm sure we will.

Questions

1. Do you think the concert tickets are reasonably priced?
2. Is it better to sit in the orchestra section or to buy a general admission ticket?
3. Why might John have chosen the seats on the end rather than in the middle?
4. What time do you think they should arrive for the event?

Buying Tickets

The Best Seat in the House

Individual seating preferences may vary. However, to ensure the best possible viewing experience, it is recommended to have **a 36-degree viewing angle** from the farthest seat in the auditorium.

If you want to get the best audio experience, you should sit about two-thirds of the way back from the screen, in a seat one or two away from the exact center.

Questions

Q1. Do you have a certain seating preference?

Q2. Where do you usually sit at a movie theater?

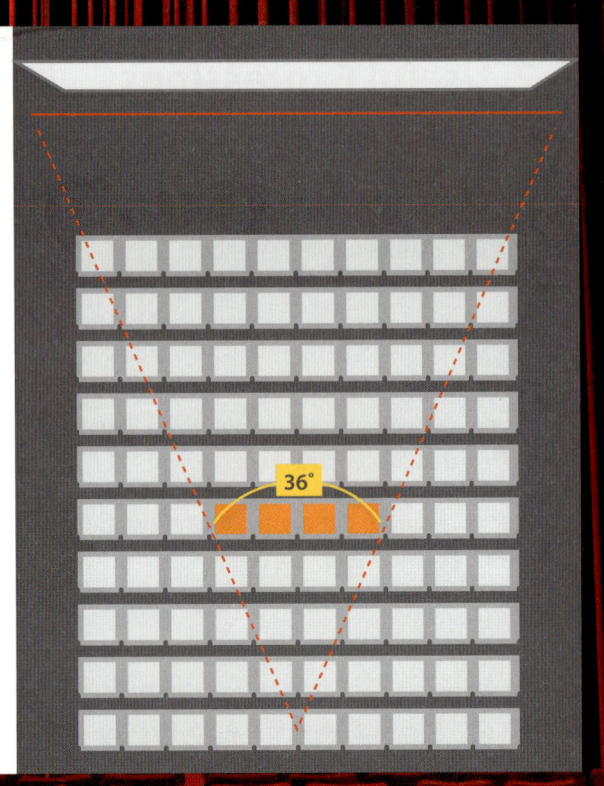

4. Language Practice

Using the key words, complete the sentences then practice making your own sentences.

Practice #1 — Checking availability

- 9:00 show / Saturday
- piano concert / May 12th
- musical / weekend

★ Do you have any tickets available for the _____ _____ on _____?

★ Is the _____ sold out for _____?

★ Can I still reserve seats for the _____ next _____?

Practice #2 — Choosing seats

- three seats / orchestra pit
- four general admission
- two / in the center

★ We want to get _____ _____ tickets.

★ I want to reserve _____ seats _____.

★ We'd like _____ in the _____, please.

Practice #3 — Getting tickets

- more convenient / online
- fast / ticketing machine
- cheaper / box office

★ It's _____ to buy movie tickets at the _____.

★ It will be _____ to get our concert tickets _____.

★ They say it's _____ to go to the _____ for play tickets.

5. Role Plays

Look at the situations and act out the role plays with your partner.

Situation #1

Role A

You are waiting in line to buy your family tickets for a musical. You need 4 tickets, including one child's ticket.

1. Ask if there are four seats available together.
2. Check the price of the tickets.
3. Request seats as close to the center as possible.

Role B

You are a cashier at a box office selling tickets for a musical. The tickets are $19.95 for adults and $10.95 for children under 12. Take the customer's order and answer his questions.

1. Tell the customer that there are a lot of seats still available.
2. Ask how many tickets and tell the customer the price.
3. Ask where the customer would like to be seated.

Situation #2

Role A

You want to buy movie tickets for you and your friend for the 5:00 show. You would like to sit in the center of the theater in the middle.

1. Ask for two tickets in the center.
2. Agree to take the seats in the back.
3. Say you will pay by credit card.

Role B

You are working at a movie theater. The 5:00 show is almost sold out and there are only two seats together in the back. Help a customer buy tickets for the movie.

1. Tell the customer the only seats together are in the back.
2. Ask how the customer will be paying.
3. Thank the customer for his or her business.

Situational Collocations!

Look at the collocations and try making your own sentences.

valid ticket	You must hold a valid ticket before boarding the train.
base price	The base price was set at 20 dollars.
steeper price	Special theaters like 3D theaters have steeper prices.
get scammed	I almost got scammed into buying fake tickets.
annual pass	I bought an annual pass for Disney World.
front row tickets	I won front row tickets to a NBA finals game!
seating chart	We need to check our seats on the seating chart.
fully occupied	All seats are fully occupied.

1.
2.

Buying Tickets

BOX OFFICE

1. The box office is a place at theaters, concert halls, and exhibitions where tickets are bought or reserved. It is also known as a ticket booth.

2. The term box office is also used to indicate the degree of success of movies and films. It's measured by the amount of money the film has earned by ticket sales.

    e.g.) Avatar has the world's top box office hit of $2,787,956,087 followed by Titanic at $2,186,772,302.

6. Cultural Discussion Questions

Talk about the questions in as much detail as possible.

1. Is it easy to buy movie or concert tickets in your country? How do you purchase them?
2. Do you often have to wait in line for tickets? Why or why not?
3. You bought a concert ticket, but you cannot attend the event. What are your options?
4. If you wanted to buy tickets to a sold-out event in your country, where would be the best place to look? Explain.

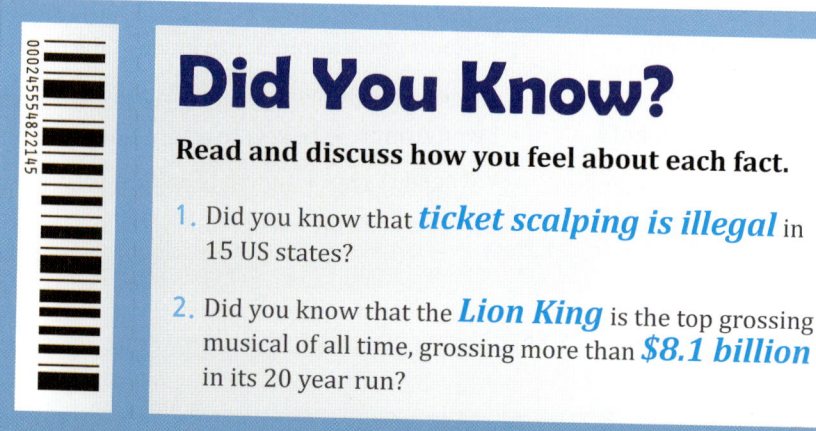

Did You Know?

Read and discuss how you feel about each fact.

1. Did you know that **ticket scalping is illegal** in 15 US states?
2. Did you know that the **Lion King** is the top grossing musical of all time, grossing more than **$8.1 billion** in its 20 year run?

7. Slang & Idioms

Match the slang phrases and idioms with their definitions and use them to complete the sentences below.

1. ___ face value
2. ___ scalper
3. ___ the pit
4. ___ front row center
5. ___ big name

A. a person who is famous in a certain sphere

B. a person who resells tickets for a large or quick profit

C. the value printed or depicted on a coin, banknote, postage stamp, or ticket

D. an area where the audience stands at the front of the stage

E. in or at the forefront of activity

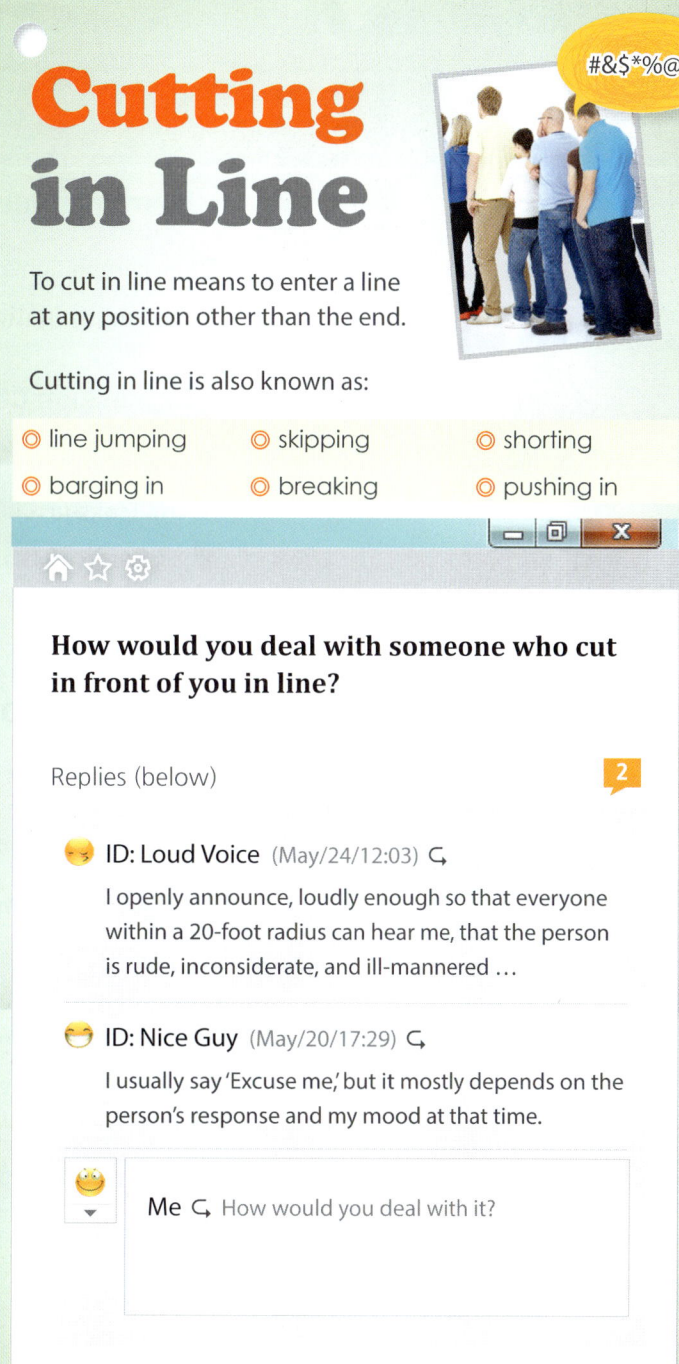

1. Do you care if we get _____ tickets or general admission?

2. I was so excited when he surprised me with _____ seats to see my favorite band.

3. A _____ just tried to sell me a ticket at twice the regular price!

4. You shouldn't pay above _____ for a ticket.

5. She's a _____, so her shows should sell out fast.

Wrapping Up!

Write down four things you learned from this lesson and review.

06 Congratulations!

» Learning Objective

Upon completion of this lesson, you will be able to...
offer congratulations on the birth of a child.

» Expression Check

- ☑ He is as cute as a button.
- ☑ He looks just like his father!
- ☑ How are mother and baby doing?

1. Warm Up Activity

Describe what is happening in the picture.

Talk about the questions.

1. Do you have any children? If so, describe what they looked like when they were babies.
2. Do you enjoy meeting babies? Why or why not?
3. What do people usually say to congratulate new parents in your country?

Lesson 06 / Congratulations! **41**

2. Useful Expressions

Match the expressions (a-d) to its similar meaning (1-4).

A He's as cute as a button. ★ ★ 1 Her eyes look just like her father's.

B He keeps me up all night. ★ ★ 2 She took some time off work to have a baby.

C She went on maternity leave. ★ ★ 3 He's so adorable.

D She has her father's eyes. ★ ★ 4 He makes me stay awake all night.

3. Key Conversation

Think of the useful expressions and practice the dialogue.

Welcome to the World…

Angie	Hey Mom. Would you mind helping with the baby?
Carol	Not at all. He's as cute as a button. Who could resist such a cute little baby?
Angie	He seems to like you.
Carol	It's a mother's touch, I guess. Speaking of which, how are mother and baby doing?
Angie	Busy and exhausted. He keeps me up all night. At least I have Paul here to help out a bit.
Carol	Well, that's good. Paul is such a good man for you.
Angie	Yeah, I think so, too.
Carol	Welcome to the world, little one. Oh, look! He's smiling! How adorable.
Angie	He has his daddy's smile.
Carol	You know? I think so, too – but he has your eyes.
Angie	You think so?

Questions

1. Do you think Carol is good with children?
2. Why do you think Angie needs help with the baby?
3. Do you think Paul and Angie will make good parents?
4. How does Angie's baby resemble his parents?

Congratulations!

Who Do You Look Like More?

Do you think that we are 50% like our mother and 50% like our father? It is true that we inherited half of our DNA from each parent, but that does not mean that the end product is 50-50. Think about who you look like more and describe how you resemble your parents.

 Mother   Father   Relatives (other than my parents)

I have my mother's eyes. My nose looks just like my father's.

4. Language Practice

Using the key words, complete the sentences then practice making your own sentences.

Practice #1 — Expressing feelings

- How are mother and baby doing?
- He's as cute as a button.
- She looks so much like you!

★ A: This is my newborn daughter, Jessica.
  B: _____

★ A: Come and look at your new nephew!
  B: _____

★ A: I just visited Susan in the hospital.
  B: _____

Practice #2 — Talking about a baby

- mother's eyes
- adorable face
- sleep through

★ Is he _____ the night yet?

★ She has her _____.

★ What an _____!

Practice #3 — Asking about a baby

- When will you bring him in for us to meet?
- How old is the baby now?
- When do you get to take her home?

★ A: _____
  B: We just need to spend a few more days in the hospital.

★ A: My sister had a baby.
  B: _____

★ A: Our son was born last weekend!
  B: _____

5. Role Plays

Look at the situations and act out the role plays with your partner.

Situation #1

Role A

A friend has invited you to a baby shower for his or her new baby. You are excited to see the baby and your friend. Congratulate him or her and make conversation about the new addition to his or her family.

1. Congratulate your friend and tell how happy you are to be there.
2. Compliment the baby.
3. Ask how the new parents are doing.

Role B

You just had a son two weeks ago! The baby has not been sleeping well and you are very tired but happy. Talk to a guest at the baby shower.

1. Thank your friend for coming.
2. Tell about how happy you are with your new child.
3. Mention how the baby has not been sleeping.

Situation #2

Role A

You and your spouse just had a new baby. You brought the baby to work today to show him off to your colleagues.

1. Introduce the baby to your co-workers by name.
2. Tell about how happy you are to have a child.
3. Say that you need to get the baby home soon.

Role B

Your teammate just had a baby. Make conversation about the baby when he or she brings him into the office.

1. Congratulate your teammate on the baby's birth.
2. Ask how your teammate has been doing.
3. Say you can't wait to see the baby and your co-worker again soon.

Situational Collocations!

Look at the collocations and try making your own sentences.

new addition	Congratulations on the new addition to the family!
only child	I have no siblings – I am the only child.
rock the baby	Dave, can you rock the baby to sleep?
sleepless nights	Even if our baby gave us so many sleepless nights, I don't regret it.
maternity leave	The company was generous enough to give me an extended maternity leave.
paternity leave	My paternity leave starts right when my wife's maternity leave ends.
give birth	When did you give birth to your second?
expect a baby	My best friend is expecting a baby in June.

1. ....

2. ....

Congratulations!

How to Be a Good Parent

Being a parent is one of the most fulfilling experiences a person can have. The most important thing a parent can give their child, however, is a sense of being loved. Just keep in mind that you do not have to be infallible to be a "perfect" parent.

1 Express Your Love and Affection
Tell them you love them every day and give lots of hugs and kisses.

2 Praise Your Children
Avoid comparing your children to others. Each child is individual and unique.

3 Be Consistent
If you give them a punishment, be sure they understand the reason and the fault.

4 Be a Role Model
Young kids are like sponges: they notice everything. Do not forget you are your children's first role model.

5 Eliminate Bad Habits
Pay attention to what you say or do around them and think about what kind of example you are setting.

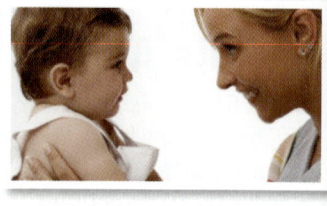

The Science of Bonding
"Maternal Affection"

According to a journal, high levels of maternal affection during early infancy create secure attachments and bonding that will help children cope with life's stressors even as adults.

6. Cultural Discussion Questions

Talk about the questions in as much detail as possible.

1. How long is maternity leave in your country?
2. Where do women usually give birth in your country? Do they prefer to go home after birth or stay somewhere else?
3. Is it common in your country for women to have a baby shower before they have a new baby?
4. Do you think it is necessary for a mother to stay home with her baby? Why or why not?

Did You Know?

Read and discuss how you feel about each fact.

1. Did you know that a *two-day-old baby can recognize* his or her mother's voice from a recording?
2. Did you know that *babies do not cry tears for at least three weeks* after they are born?

How Fast Does a Baby Grow?

The term "baby" refers to any child from birth to age four. A "newborn" is a baby that is less than three months of age. "Infants" are babies from three months to one year old. "Toddlers" are babies from one year to four years of age.

7. Slang & Idioms

Match the slang phrases and idioms with their definitions and use them to complete the sentences below.

1. ___ baby bump
2. ___ bundle of joy
3. ___ baby shower
4. ___ with child
5. ___ sleep like a baby

A. a newborn baby
B. to sleep soundly
C. pregnant
D. the protruding stomach of a woman who is visibly pregnant
E. a gift-giving party to celebrate the delivery or expected birth of a child

1. My son seems really excited now, but tonight I know he'll _____.
2. You're expected to bring a gift if you're invited to a _____.
3. I can't believe you already gave birth! The last time I saw you, you barely had a _____.
4. So, how old is your little _____?
5. How long has your wife been _____?

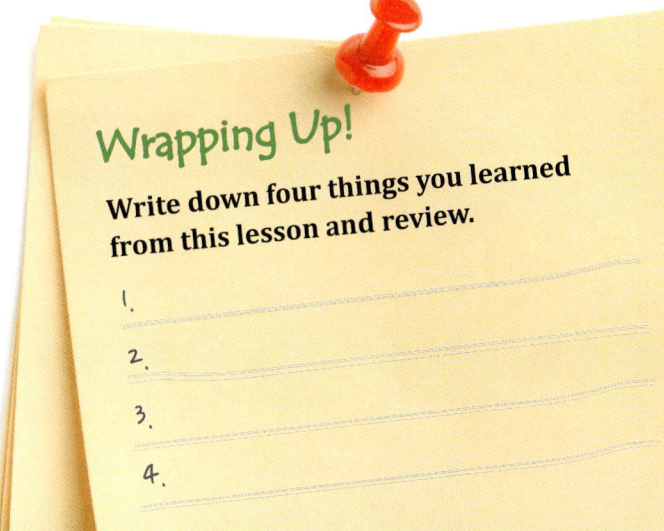

Wrapping Up!
Write down four things you learned from this lesson and review.

1.
2.
3.
4.

Volunteer Work

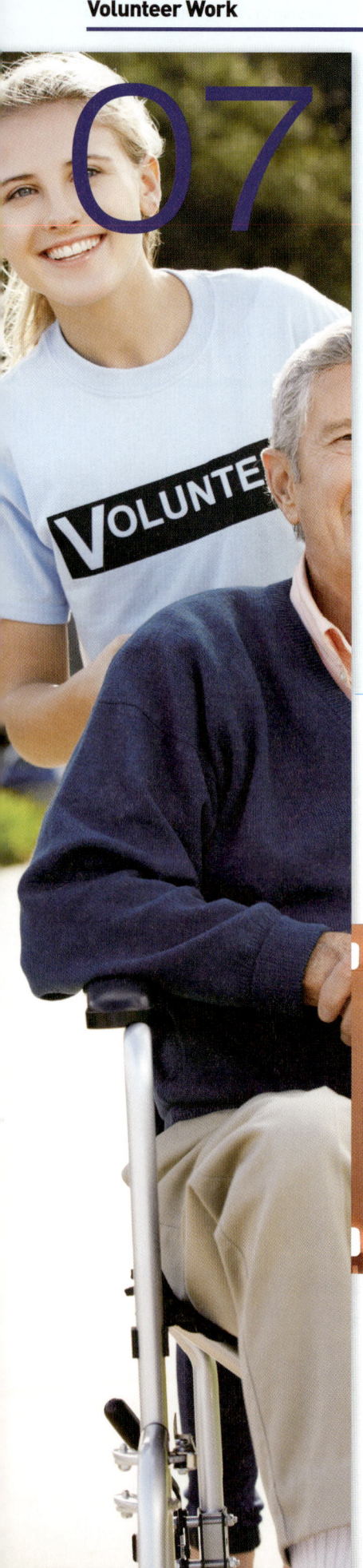

Volunteer Work

07

» **Learning Objective**

Upon completion of this lesson, you will be able to...

describe and discuss volunteer experiences with others.

» **Expression Check**

- ☑ I'd like to give back to the community.
- ☑ I just want to make a difference.
- ☑ Could you lend a hand here?

1. Warm Up Activity

Describe what is happening in the picture.

Talk about the questions.

1. Would you like to work as a volunteer?
2. How often do you volunteer your time to an important cause?
3. What kind of volunteer work can you do in your city?

2. Useful Expressions

Match the expressions (a-d) to its similar meaning (1-4).

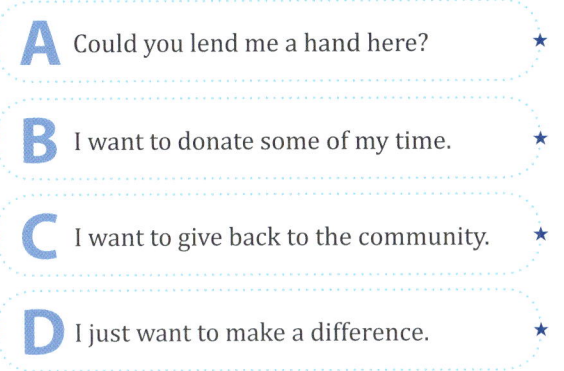

3. Key Conversation

 Think of the useful expressions and practice the dialogue.

Something I Believe in

Rachel	Hi, Peter. How are those signs coming for the food drive next week?
Peter	Pretty good, but there's still a lot to do. Could you lend me a hand here?
Rachel	Sure, no problem. I'm sure that if we work together, we can get them done much faster.
Peter	So, how often do you come to help out at the center?
Rachel	Once or twice a week.
Peter	Oh, really? Why do you come that often? I only come maybe once a month.
Rachel	I enjoy giving my time to something I believe in. Plus, I want to make a difference in people's lives.
Peter	That's very noble of you. I think I should give more of my time, too.
Rachel	You should. We could use the help around here.
Peter	Where do I sign up?

Questions

1. Where do you think Rachel and Peter are volunteering?
2. Who do you think will get the food from the food drive?
3. Do you think Rachel likes volunteering her time?
4. How often do Peter and Rachel volunteer?

Volunteer Work

Interesting *Volunteer* Work Opportunities

Volunteering provides people with the opportunity to learn new skills that can be used to further their careers later in life. Here are some types of volunteer work for students.

1. Teaching children
2. Planting trees
3. Helping to preserve the environment
4. Helping to feed homeless and poverty-stricken people
5. Caring for animals that are homeless or have some sort of injury
6. Aiding in the construction of new schools, homes, or playgrounds

DID YOU KNOW?

- More than 264 million children worldwide do not have access to schools or are not able to attend due to financial reasons.
- Only 83 percent of the children who start school at all complete elementary school, and just 45 percent of students aged 15 to 17 will finish secondary school.

4. Language Practice

Using the key words, complete the sentences then practice making your own sentences.

Practice #1 — Volunteer organizations

- food bank
- homeless shelter
- soup kitchen

★ People who do not have a place to stay can sleep at a _____.

★ We serve food to the poor at a _____.

★ Many people donate food to a _____.

Practice #2 — Volunteer work

- garbage / park
- elderly / hospice
- dogs / animal shelter

★ She goes to care for the _____ at the _____.

★ They visited the _____ at the _____.

★ On Saturdays, we pick up _____ in the _____.

Practice #3 — Asking about volunteering

- who will benefit from
- take place
- information

★ Could I have some _____ about volunteer opportunities?

★ Where will the event _____?

★ _____ the food drive?

5. Role Plays

Look at the situations and act out the role plays with your partner.

Role A

You are trying to gather a team of volunteers from your neighborhood to help clean up a local park between 10:00 a.m. and 1:00 p.m. next Saturday. Ask one of your neighbors if he or she would be interested in helping.

1. Invite your neighbor to the event.
2. Give information about when and where the event will be held.
3. Ask if your neighbor knows anyone else who would want to participate.

Role B — Situation #1

Your neighbor is asking for help cleaning up garbage at a local park.
Ask questions to find out more about the event.

1. Check when and where the event will be taking place.
2. Agree to volunteer on Saturday.
3. Promise to invite some friends.

Role A

You and a friend are talking over lunch. You are telling him or her about an enjoyable experience volunteering in a soup kitchen a few days ago. You served food to the homeless and met many nice people.

1. Tell about the work you did.
2. Explain how helping made you feel.
3. Invite your friend to join you next time.

Role B — Situation #2

You are having lunch with your friend. Ask your friend about his or her recent experience volunteering at a soup kitchen.

1. Ask what kind of work he or she did.
2. Ask if he or she enjoyed it.
3. Agree to go with your friend next time.

Situational Collocations!

Look at the collocations and try making your own sentences.

get involved	Encourage her to get involved in fund-raising for charity.
made a donation	He made a generous donation to the charity.
charity event	The charity event had an even greater turnout than expected.
community service	Community service is the meat and potatoes of this program.
raise money	Our church held a flea market to raise money for flood victims.
put aside	I put some time aside every week to do volunteer work.
nursing home	Her family put her into a nursing home.
humbling experience	Helping the needy is an unbelievably humbling experience.

1.
2.

Volunteer Work

6. Cultural Discussion Questions

Talk about the questions in as much detail as possible.

1. Do you think the benefits of volunteering are worth the time and effort that it requires?
2. Do people in your country volunteer very often?
3. Have you ever volunteered? Tell about your experience.
4. What are some things that you can do to help people in your local community? Be specific.

Reasons to Volunteer Abroad

Have you ever taken part in volunteer work abroad?
Why did you apply for the volunteer work?
Put a check mark beside the most important reason for you.

☐ **Internal Rewards**
The promise of feeling good about yourself for helping others is one of the most popular reasons to volunteer abroad. Many developing countries do not have the resources for things we take for granted. For example, adequate numbers of doctors and sophisticated medical facilities are rare in many areas of Africa. Regardless of your profession, you can contribute to a better way of life for these people by offering skills you may have.

☐ **Resume Building**
Many college students choose to volunteer abroad because it looks good on their resumes.

☐ **Gaining Experience and Skills**
Volunteer organizations typically train you to perform specific tasks in the host country. You gain valuable knowledge and skills that can help you in your current profession or prepare you for a new one.

☐ **Learning a Foreign Language**
Many organizations that have volunteer positions abroad teach survival language skills.

Did You Know?

Read and discuss how you feel about each fact.

 1. Did you know that **volunteerism** has a value of over **$184 billion**?

2. Did you know that there are more than **1.8 million** active **nonprofits** in the United States alone?

Volunteer Quotes

Volunteering means working together for the simple common goal of improving the quality of life for others. Get inspired to volunteer with this selection of quotes about the topic.

We make a living by what we get; we make a life by what we give.
~Winston Churchill

Volunteers do not necessarily have the time; they just have the heart.
~Elizabeth Andrew

The best way to find yourself is to lose yourself in the service of others.
~Gandhi

A candle loses nothing of its light when lighting another.
~Kahlil Gibran

All that we send into the lives of others comes back into our own.
~Anonymous

Volunteers are paid in six figures... S-M-I-L-E-S.
~Gayla LeMaire

7. Slang & Idioms

Match the slang phrases and idioms with their definitions and use them to complete the sentences below.

1. ___ for a good cause
2. ___ actions speak louder than words
3. ___ take the credit
4. ___ pay it forward
5. ___ nonprofit

A. an organization not making or conducted primarily to make a profit
B. to be worth doing or giving to because it will help other people
C. to respond to a person's kindness by being kind to someone else
D. to allow people to believe that one did something that deserves praise
E. what you do shows your intentions more than what you say

1. The best places to volunteer are _____ organizations.
2. I can't _____. It was a group effort.
3. I'm always happy to help if it's _____.
4. You always talk about the importance of charity, but never do anything. _____!
5. When someone helps you with something important, it is good to _____ and help someone else in need.

Wrapping Up!

Write down four things you learned from this lesson and review.

1.
2.
3.
4.

TGIF

» Learning Objective

Upon completion of this lesson, you will be able to...

express excitement about the weekend.

» Expression Check

- ☑ I can't wait for this day to be over!
- ☑ I'm counting down the minutes to the weekend.
- ☑ I'm hoping to knock off early today.

1. Warm Up Activity

Describe what is happening in the picture.

Talk about the questions.

1. How do you plan your weekend activities?
2. Do you enjoy spending a "lazy weekend" at home, or do you prefer to "get away from it all"?
3. Are there any special things that you usually wait for the weekend to do?

2. Useful Expressions

Match the expressions (a-d) to its similar meaning (1-4).

A I hear you.

B I can't wait to knock off early.

C Where are you headed?

D It's been a long week.

1 Where are you going?

2 This week has seemed endless.

3 I agree with you.

4 I'm looking forward to finishing work early.

3. Key Conversation

Think of the useful expressions and practice the dialogue.

I Need a Change of Scenery

Lisa	Hey, how're things?
Larry	Not too bad, now that it's finally Friday.
Lisa	I hear you! This week has seemed endless.
Larry	I can't wait for this day to be over. Are you going out tonight? After all, we deserve a bit of fun!
Lisa	My boyfriend is picking me up after work, and we're going out for dinner and a movie. How about you?
Larry	I can't wait to knock off early and hop on a train to get away from it all!
Lisa	Great! Where are you headed?
Larry	Anywhere—I need a change of scenery. Hopefully, I'll be out of here by four this afternoon!
Lisa	Sounds good!
Larry	Yeah, I'm counting down the minutes until the time I can leave.
Lisa	Have a great weekend. See you on Monday!

Questions

1. Who do you think will enjoy their weekend more?
2. Do you think Lisa is looking forward to the evening?
3. Do you think Larry has a good idea?
4. Do you think Lisa and Larry like their jobs?

TGIF

Black Friday

Black Friday is the day following Thanksgiving Day in the United States (4th Thursday in November), traditionally the beginning of the Christmas shopping season. On this day, most major retailers open extremely early, often at 4 a.m. or earlier, and offer promotional sales to kick off the shopping season, similar to Boxing Day sales in many Commonwealth Nations. Black Friday is not actually a holiday, but some non-retail employers give their employees the day off, increasing the number of potential shoppers.

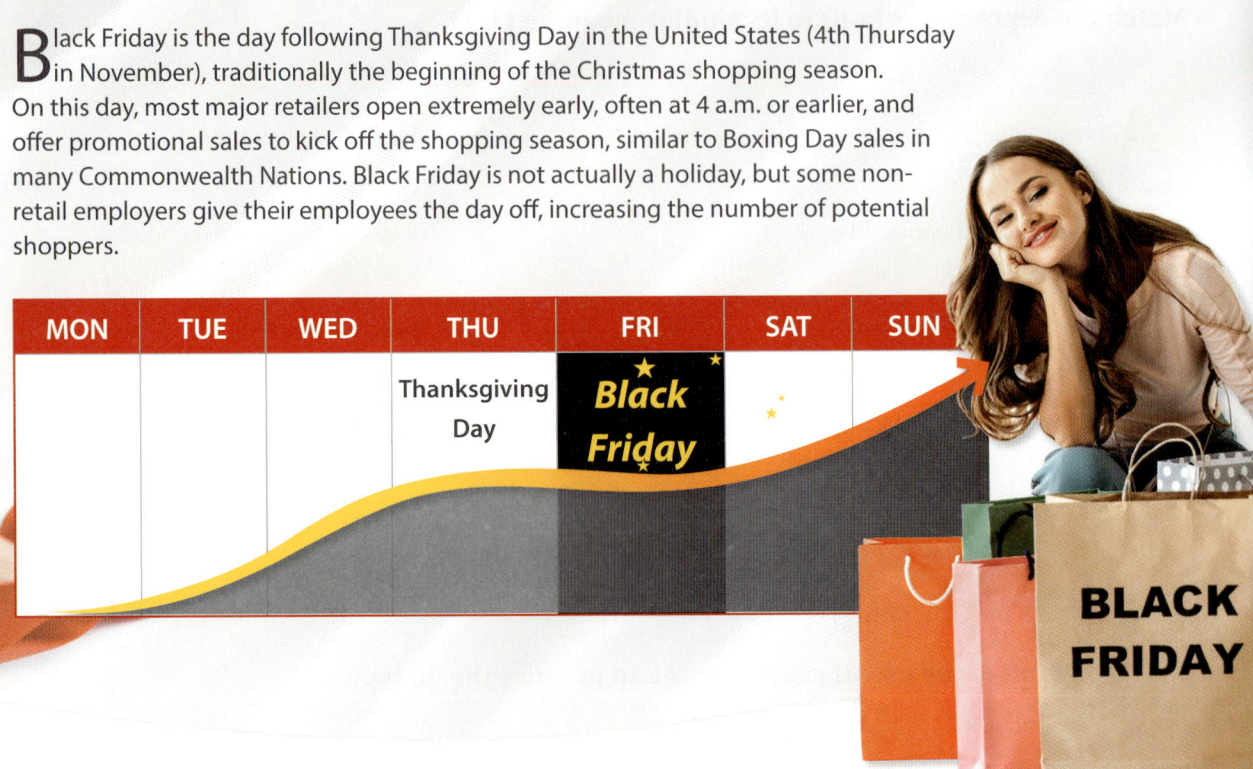

4. Language Practice

Using the key words, complete the sentences then practice making your own sentences.

Practice #1 — Discussing plans

- this weekend
- after work on Friday
- Saturday night

★ What are your plans for _____?

★ What are you getting up to _____?

★ Are you looking forward to the party _____?

Practice #2 — Suggesting getaway plans

- get away from it all
- dinner and a movie
- knock off early

★ How about _____ _____ today?

★ How do you feel about _____?

★ Do you want to _____ _____ this weekend?

Practice #3 — Looking forward to the future

- counting down the minutes
- can't wait
- relax and take it easy

★ I _____ to get out of here.

★ She's _____ _____ to her birthday.

★ He's hoping to _____ _____ this weekend.

5. Role Plays

Look at the situations and act out the role plays with your partner.

Situation #1

Role A
You are really excited about a camping trip that you have planned for this weekend. You are going to go hiking in the mountains with your friends. Tell your co-worker about your weekend plans.

1. Ask your co-worker about his or her plans.
2. Talk about what you are going to do.
3. Explain how excited you are.

Role B
You are discussing weekend plans with your co-worker. You plan to take it easy at home.

1. Tell your co-worker about your plans.
2. Ask about his or her plans for the weekend.
3. Ask a backup question about your co-worker's plan.

Role A
Next Monday is a public holiday. You don't have any plans for the long weekend. Call up a friend and plan a short weekend getaway together.

1. Ask your friend about his or her plans.
2. Suggest doing something together.
3. Plan when and where to meet.

Role B
Your friend calls and asks about your plans for the three-day weekend. You don't have any yet but heard about a music festival in another city. Suggest going together.

1. Say that you have no plans.
2. Suggest going to the music festival.
3. Ask if your friend wants to go in your car.

Situation #2

Situational Collocations!

Look at the collocations and try making your own sentences.

quality time	How about we spend some quality time this weekend?
come by	Do you guys want to come by my house this Sunday?
stay indoors	I'm planning to stay indoors all weekend, had a rough week.
headed home	I'm headed home right after work, no partying for me.
family night	Sunday night is always family night.
community sports	I participate in local community sports whenever I can.
free time	Ever since we got our second child, I don't even get free time on weekends.
take lessons	I take piano lessons on the weekend.

1.
2.

TGIF

Weekly Sleep Diary

Check three boxes in the appropriate places on the chart below and compare how many hours you sleep each day.

● Wake-up Time   △ Time You Arrive at Home   ★ Time You Go to Sleep

	Mon	Tue	Wed	Thu	Fri	Sat	Sun
04:00							
06:00							
08:00							
10:00							
12:00							
14:00							
16:00							
18:00							
20:00							
22:00							
24:00							
02:00							
04:00							

Q1. Do you often take naps? How long do you nap for?
Q2. Do you often get up in the middle of the night?

6. Cultural Discussion Questions

Talk about the questions in as much detail as possible.

1. Do you think most people look forward to the weekend?
2. Is it common for people from your country to go somewhere to get away from it all?
3. What kind of activities do most people do on the weekend in your country?
4. In many countries, Friday is the end of the working week and often payday. How about in your country?

Did You Know?

Read and discuss how you feel about each fact.

1. Did you know that the term TGIF was originated by Jerry Healy, an Akron, Ohio disk jockey *on radio station* WAKR in the *early 1970s*?

2. Did you know that workplaces in many Western countries have *"Casual Friday"*? This is a day when employees don't need to dress professionally and can come to work in jeans and a t-shirt if they want.

Why "Man Friday"?

Man Friday is a character in the book Robinson Crusoe. He is a native man who becomes Crusoe's servant friend after Crusoe saves him from being killed by people who eat other people. Crusoe calls him "Man Friday" because he meets him on Friday.
Now, we call a person who does many different types of uninteresting work in an office a "girl/man/person Friday."

Friday the 13th

Friday the 13th is a date considered to be bad luck in Western superstition. An estimated 17 to 21 million people in the US are affected by a fear of this day, making it the most feared day and date in history. Some people are so paralyzed by fear that they avoid their normal routines in doing business, taking flights, or even getting out of bed. It has been estimated that $800 to $900 million is lost in business on this day.

7. Slang & Idioms

Match the slang phrases and idioms with their definitions and use them to complete the sentences below.

1. ___ chomping at the bit
2. ___ fired up
3. ___ bouncing off the walls
4. ___ watching the clock
5. ___ just around the corner

A. to be very excited and anxious about an upcoming event
B. to be full of nervous excitement or agitation
C. very close in time or distance
D. to be overwhelmingly excited
E. to keep looking at what the time is, usually because you are eager to leave

1. She was happy at work on Friday knowing that the weekend was _____.
2. It's only Thursday but John is already _____ thinking about the long weekend.
3. Mary was _____ to get out of the office on Friday afternoon.
4. She was so excited about the weekend getaway that on Friday she was _____.
5. As the weekend drew near, the children were _____.

Wrapping Up!
Write down four things you learned from this lesson and review.

1. _____
2. _____
3. _____
4. _____

09 Grabbing a Drink

» Learning Objective

Upon completion of this lesson, you will be able to...

make plans with colleagues after work.

» Expression Check

- ☑ Are you up for drinks after work today?
- ☑ You don't have to ask me twice.
- ☑ I'm sure you can twist my arm.

1. Warm Up Activity

Describe what is happening in the picture.

Talk about the questions.

1. How often do you go out for drinks with your co-workers?
2. What do people in your country generally do after work?
3. What type of places do you enjoy going with your colleagues?

2. Useful Expressions

Match the expressions (a-d) to its similar meaning (1-4).

A You don't have to ask me twice.

B Would you like to swing by for a drink?

C Can I bring another round for you guys?

D Are you up for drinks after work today?

1 Are you interested in having a drink at my place?

2 Are you interested in going out for drinks after work?

3 Would anyone like more to drink?

4 I'm interested. Let's go!

3. Key Conversation

Think of the useful expressions and practice the dialogue.

A Chance to Unwind

Rachel	Hey Beth.
Beth	Oh, hey Rachel. How did the presentation go?
Rachel	I don't know. I hope I did OK.
Beth	Hey, Sarah and I were thinking of celebrating her new promotion. You want to join us?
Rachel	What are you doing?
Beth	We were thinking of going to Moe's for a few drinks to toast her.
Rachel	Well, I'm sure you could twist my arm a bit.
Beth	Great! We're meeting back here at 7:30.
Rachel	OK. I'll be here.
Beth	Awesome. See you tonight.
Rachel	Yeah, see you then.

Questions

1. Do you think Rachel did well on her presentation?
2. Do you think Rachel wants to go out with Beth and Sarah?
3. How would you celebrate a co-worker's promotion?
4. Do you think the women will enjoy themselves?

Grabbing a Drink

Countries by Alcohol Consumption

Muslims make up roughly **97%** of Pakistan's population, so it is only the **3%** minority who are eligible to buy alcohol with a permit in Pakistan.

On the other hand, Belarusians have the highest per capita consumption of alcohol in the world, consuming 17.5 liters per person every year. For comparison, the world average consumption is only 6.2 liters. Hard liquor is most popular among Belarusians (47% of consumption), while beer makes up only 17% and wine only 5%. The remaining 30% is cheap fruit wines (plonk) and homemade vodka, called Samahon.

Pakistan
0.06 liters per person/year

South Korea
12.3 liters per person/year

Belarus
17.5 liters per person/year

Q1. What is your favorite alcoholic beverage?
Q2. When was the last time you had a drink? What did you drink?

4. Language Practice
Using the key words, complete the sentences then practice making your own sentences.

Practice #1 — Inviting

- grab a drink
- another round
- drop by

★ Could I interest you guys in _____?

★ Do you want to _____ later for a drink?

★ Anyone want to _____ _____ after work?

Practice #2 — Answering

- after work
- whatever's on tap
- promotion

★ A: What can I get you to drink?
B: I'd like a beer. I'll take _____.

★ A: What's the occasion?
B: I just got a _____.

★ A: When should I meet you?
B: Let's meet up _____.

Practice #3 — Confirming plans

- come along
- at / in
- stop by

★ Meet me _____ Bay Station _____ 20 minutes.

★ He will _____ to Moe's with us.

★ _____ my place tonight.

5. Role Plays

Look at the situations and act out the role plays with your partner.

Situation #1

Role A
Your manager is inviting everyone for a drink. You would like to go, but you have already made plans with a friend. Give an excuse to your manager.

1. Thank your manager for inviting you.
2. Explain why you can't come.
3. Promise to come along next time.

Role B
You are a department manager and you would like your employees to get together for drinks tonight. Invite one of your employees out.

1. Ask your employee to come out for drinks tonight.
2. Accept the excuse.
3. Tell the employee that you will give him or her more notice next time.

Situation #2

Role A
You just found out that you received a promotion! Invite one of your team members out to celebrate.

1. Ask about your team member's plans for tonight.
2. Invite him or her out.
3. Decide on a place to go together.

Role B
Your teammate invites you out to celebrate his or her promotion. Accept the invitation and suggest a place to go.

1. Say you don't have any plans.
2. Accept the invitation and congratulate your co-worker.
3. Suggest a place that you would like to go.

Situational Collocations!

Look at the collocations and try making your own sentences.

after work drinks	Anybody up for some after work drinks?
loosen up	Let's go get some drinks and loosen up this environment.
round of drinks	Great job with the project team! First round of drinks are on me!
pint of beer	I can come along for just one pint of beer.
few drinks	We're going to go grab a few drinks after work. Want to tag along?
non-alcoholic drinks	I'm on meds right now, so I can only drink non-alcoholic drinks.
relieve stress	We're planning to get some drinks after work to relieve stress.
designated driver	I'm going as the designated driver, so no alcohol for me.

1.
2.

Grabbing a Drink

A Brief Guide to Alcoholic Glasses

Different drinks call for different glasses. Look at the pictures and explain what kind of beverage each glass is used for.

When do you use each glass?

Draw the special shape of the glass used for the local alcohol in your country. Then, describe it.

Answer: (1) Wine (2) Beer (3) Cocktail (4) Whisky

6. Cultural Discussion Questions

Talk about the questions in as much detail as possible.

1. If you go out for drinks with your colleagues, how do you usually decide who pays?
2. What is the best day of the week to go out for drinks after work?
3. How do you feel about drinking in your culture?
4. Do you feel that your company's corporate culture encourages drinking? Why or why not?

Did You Know?

Read and discuss how you feel about each fact.

1. Did you know that in the UK, children *5 years old* and older *can legally drink alcohol* at home or in other private locations?

2. Did you know *61%* of countries have set the *minimum legal drinking age* (MLDA) at *18 or 19 years old*? The *United States* and 11 other countries where it is legal to drink have an MLDA of *21 years old*.

Lesson 09 / Grabbing a Drink

I can drink anyone under the table.

Mr. John drank like a fish. He was a heavy drinker.

♣ **Drink like a fish?** : To drink a lot of alcohol. To drink very heavily.

♣ **Drink (someone) under the table?** : To drink more alcohol than (someone).

Q1. Do you know anyone who drinks like a fish?

Q2. Is there anyone you can drink under the table? Who is it?

7. Slang & Idioms

Match the slang phrases and idioms with their definitions and use them to complete the sentences below.

1. ___ hungover
2. ___ buzzkill
3. ___ wasted
4. ___ last call
5. ___ on the house

A. under the influence of alcohol
B. suffering from a hangover after drinking alcohol
C. a drink or meal in a bar or restaurant at the management's expense; free
D. a person or thing that has a depressing effect
E. closing time is approaching and any further drinks should be purchased immediately

1. Oh man! What a _____!
   Let's get out of here.

2. We ordered another round of drinks when the bartender rung the bell for _____.

3. Whenever my old college friends and I get together, we always end up getting _____.

4. The bartender gave everyone drinks _____ _____ to celebrate the winning team.

5. Patrick is really _____. He could barely get out of bed.

Wrapping Up!

Write down four things you learned from this lesson and review.

1.
2.
3.
4.

10 Borrowing Money

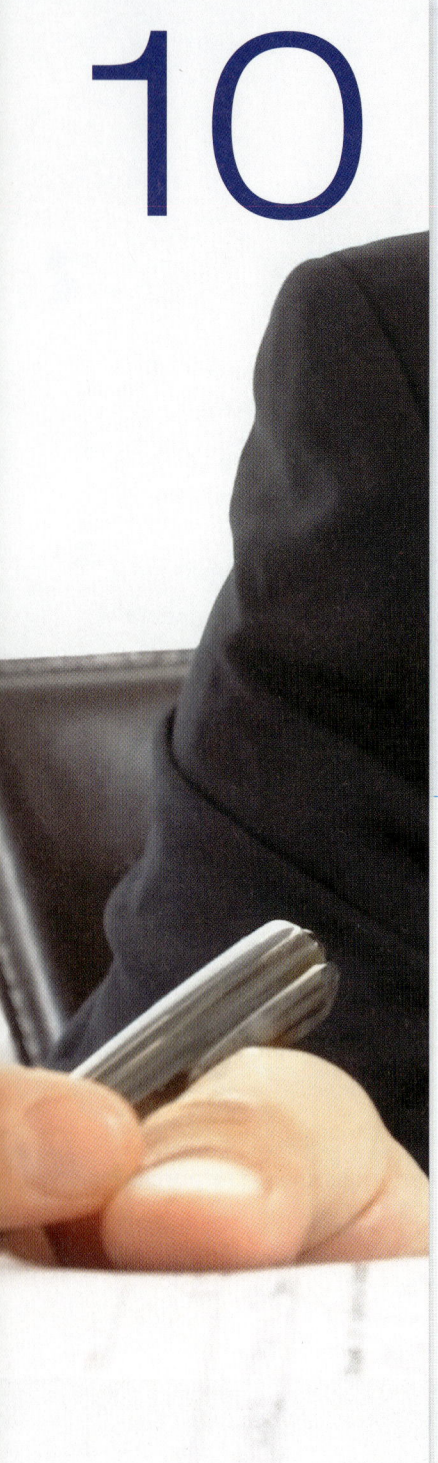

» **Learning Objective**

Upon completion of this lesson, you will be able to...

go to a bank and apply for a personal loan.

» **Expression Check**

- ☑ I'd like to apply for a personal loan.
- ☑ Why do you need the loan?
- ☑ What kind of rates can you offer me?

1. Warm Up Activity

Describe what is happening in the picture.

Talk about the questions.

1. Have you ever applied for a loan?
2. What are some ways you can buy things when you do not have enough money?
3. What are some common reasons that people take out loans?

Lesson 10 / Borrowing Money

2. Useful Expressions

Match the expressions (a-d) to its similar meaning (1-4).

A How much do I need for the down payment?

B What kind of rates can you offer me?

C I'd prefer a fixed-rate loan.

D I need to consolidate my debts.

1 How much interest do I need to pay for this loan?

2 I want to combine all of my debts into one payment.

3 How much do I have to pay up front?

4 I don't want the interest rate to change.

3. Key Conversation

Think of the useful expressions and practice the dialogue.

Shouldn't Be a Problem

James Hello, may I help you?

Erica Are you the loan officer here? The person at the desk sent me to your office.

James I am. James Mitchell is my name. What can I do for you today?

Erica I'm Erica Morris. I'd like to apply for a personal loan.

James OK. Have a seat. Why do you need the loan?

Erica Well, I need to replace my car.

James OK. Do you have any identification for me?

Erica Sure. I have my driver's license. Is that OK?

James Of course. How much money are you looking to borrow?

Erica Well, the cars I'm looking at are around $5,000.

James Well, your credit rating looks pretty good. $5,000 shouldn't be a problem.

Questions

1. Do you think Erica has applied for a loan before?
2. Why did James ask to see her identification?
3. What kind of car do you think Erica can buy with $5,000?
4. Do you think Erica will be approved for the loan?

Borrowing Money

Borrowing from a Friend

1 Here are useful expressions to use when you have to borrow something:

* Could you lend me ~?
* May/Could I borrow ~?

2 You can use the following expressions when you have to reject the request politely.

* Sorry, I'm afraid I can't.
* I'm afraid I can't afford that.
* I need it myself.
* I'm not allowed to.
* I don't have that kind of money.

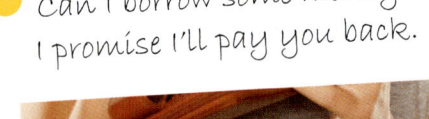
"Can I borrow some money? I promise I'll pay you back."

4. Language Practice

Using the key words, complete the sentences then practice making your own sentences.

Practice #1 — Checking details

- interest rate
- down payment
- insurance

★ What is the _____ on this loan?

★ How much does the _____ cost?

★ How much of a _____ _____ do I need?

Practice #2 — Applying

- personal loan
- student loan
- mortgage

★ Can I apply for a _____, please?

★ I'd like to take out a _____.

★ I need to apply for a _____.

Practice #3 — Personal finances

- credit score
- debt
- went broke

★ I almost _____ buying that fancy car.

★ You have an excellent _____.

★ I want to get out of _____ faster.

5. Role Plays

Look at the situations and act out the role plays with your partner.

Situation #1

Role A
Your friend just took out a loan to open a new business. You are curious about how he or she is going to pay off the loan. Ask questions to find out.

1. Ask your friend how his or her new business is doing.
2. Ask if your friend was nervous borrowing so much money.
3. Congratulate your friend on his or her success.

Role B
You just opened a successful new business. Talk to your friend about how you are paying off the loan quickly with earnings from your business. You expect to be debt free in two months.

1. Tell your friend that your business is very well.
2. Explain that you are paying off your loan quickly with the money you are making.
3. Say that you are very happy you started the business.

Situation #2

Role A
You are at the bank trying to get a loan for a new car. You need around $20,000 and have $5,000 for a down payment. Talk to a loan officer to apply for a loan.

1. Tell the loan officer what you are interested in.
2. Tell how much you need to borrow.
3. Ask about the interest rate.

Role B
You are a loan officer at a bank. Help a customer apply for a car loan. Your bank is currently offering 60-month loans at 4.0% interest.

1. Ask the customer how large of a down payment they have.
2. Explain about the conditions of the loan.
3. Ask to see the customer's ID to complete the application.

Situational Collocations!

Look at the collocations and try making your own sentences.

under pressure	The company was under pressure from not being able to pay off their loans.
poor credit	I wasn't able to apply for a loan because of my poor credit.
easy terms	My brother was able to get a large loan on easy terms.
interest rate	The private bank offered a better interest rate than the local bank.
keep afloat	Eventually I needed loans and credit cards to keep me afloat.
financial crisis	Our family got over our financial crisis by selling off our winter cabin.
monthly payment	I'll pay up for my loan through monthly payments.
prepayment penalty	Although I have the money, I shouldn't pay off all my loan because of prepayment penalties.

1.
2.

Borrowing Money

Numbers in Words

Here is a handy table showing some large numbers in words and figures. Fill in the blanks and try to read each number.

Number in Figures	Number in Words	Number in Figures	Number in Words
1,000	One thousand	1,000,000,000	One (1)
10,000	Ten thousand	10,000,000,000	Ten (2)
100,000	(3) thousand	100,000,000,000	One hundred (4)
1,000,000	One (5)	1,000,000,000,000	One (6)
10,000,000	Ten (7)	1,000,000,000,000,000	One quadrillion
100,000,000	One hundred (8)		

Answer: (1) billion (2) billion (3) One hundred (4) billion (5) million (6) trillion (7) million (8) million

Did You Know?

Read and discuss how you feel about each fact.

1. Did you know that over 44 million Americans collectively hold nearly *$1.5 trillion in student debt*?

2. Did you know excluding mortgages, Canadians carry an average of *$22,800 each in debt*?

6. Cultural Discussion Questions

Talk about the questions in as much detail as possible.

1. If you had to borrow money, would you rather pay your debt off quickly, or would you choose to just make the minimum payments? Why?

2. In your country, is it easy to get a personal loan? Why do you feel that way?

3. Is it common for people in your country to finance large purchases with credit cards?

4. Would you rather live frugally and debt free, or would you rather borrow money to support a comfortable lifestyle? Explain.

Lesson 10 / Borrowing Money **69**

"How Much Do You Need?"
How much money do you need for each of the following in your country?

Average: _____

Average: _____

Average: _____

7. Slang & Idioms

Match the slang phrases and idioms with their definitions and use them to complete the sentences below.

1. ___ two pennies to rub together
2. ___ flat broke
3. ___ break the bank
4. ___ up to my ears
5. ___ house poor

A. to have more of something than you can manage
B. spending a large proportion of one's total income on home ownership
C. to have no money
D. to not have money because something cost too much
E. to be extremely poor; to have very little money to spend

1. We are going to _____ when we get a mortgage to buy a new house.
2. Their high mortgage has made them _____.
3. I had to apply for a loan because I was _____ in debt.
4. We had to file for bankruptcy because we were _____.
5. When they first immigrated to this country, they didn't have _____.

Wrapping Up!

Write down four things you learned from this lesson and review.

The Post Office

11

The Post Office

» **Learning Objective**

Upon completion of this lesson, you will be able to...
complete tasks at the post office.

» **Expression Check**

- ☑ I have some letters to mail.
- ☑ Do you want to send it standard post or airmail?
- ☑ How long does airmail take?

1. Warm Up Activity

Describe what is happening in the picture.

Talk about the questions.

1. How often do you go to the post office?
2. What kinds of things do you usually do at the post office?
3. Is it expensive to send letters and packages in your country?

Lesson 11 / The Post Office

2. Useful Expressions

Match the expressions (a-d) to its similar meaning (1-4).

- **A** I need to drop a few letters in the mail.
- **B** Did you send the package priority mail?
- **C** How much postage do I need for this letter?
- **D** What are my choices for sending this package?

- **1** How much is it to send this letter?
- **2** How can I send this package?
- **3** I have to mail these letters.
- **4** Did you send it expedited?

3. Key Conversation

🎧 **Think of the useful expressions and practice the dialogue.**

Sending a Package

Post Office Clerk	Good afternoon. How can I help you today?
Customer	Hi. I need to send this package overseas.
Post Office Clerk	Where are you sending it to?
Customer	The UK. What are my options?
Post Office Clerk	You can send it standard mail, airmail, or priority mail.
Customer	Well, it needs to get there ASAP. How much does priority mail to the UK cost?
Post Office Clerk	Let's see. This package will cost $65 for one-day delivery or $50 for three-day.
Customer	Ouch! That's too rich for my blood. I guess I'll send it by airmail.
Post Office Clerk	OK. That will cost $43.20, and I'll make sure that it goes out tonight.
Customer	That'll be great. Thanks for your help, and have a wonderful afternoon.
Post Office Clerk	You, too!

Questions

1. Do you think the customer's package was heavy?
2. Do you think priority mail is worth the extra cost?
3. Did the customer make the right decision?
4. How would you have sent the package?

The Post Office

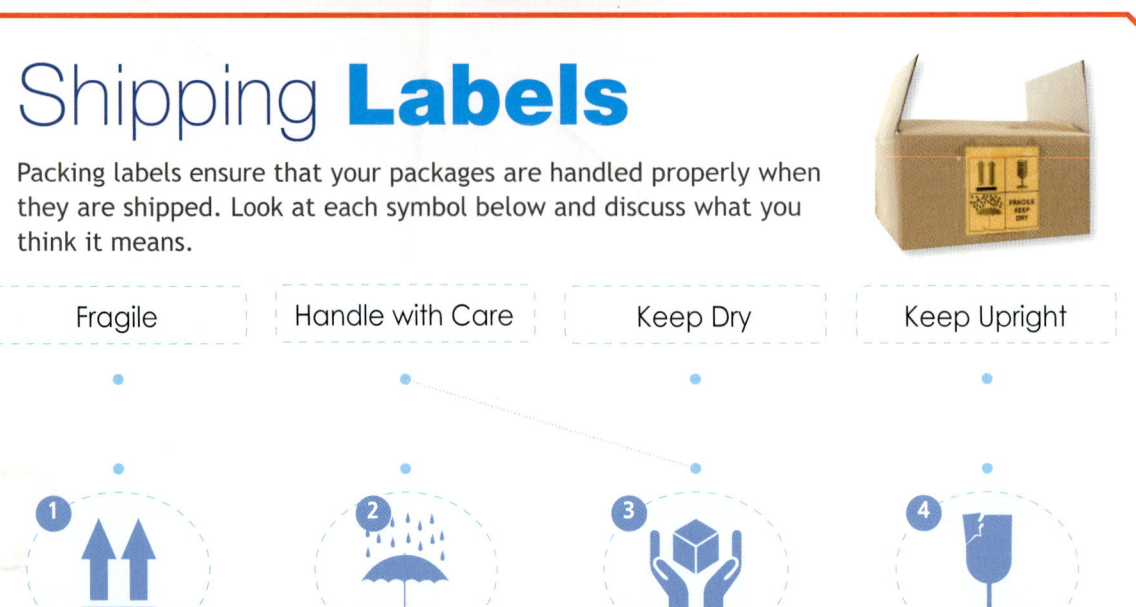

Answer: Fragile-(4) Handle with Care-(3) Keep Dry-(2) Keep Upright-(1)

4. Language Practice

Using the key words, complete the sentences then practice making your own sentences.

Practice #1 — Sending mail

- letter / airmail
- package / priority mail
- a sheet of / stamps

★ Could I send this _____ by _____, please?

★ I'd like _____ 50-cent _____.

★ Can I mail this _____ by _____, please?

Practice #2 — Confirming details

- package / the US
- letter / airmail
- document / priority mail

★ Can this _____ be sent by _____?

★ How much does it cost to send a _____ to Australia by _____?

★ How many days will the _____ take to arrive in _____?

Practice #3 — At the post office

- How would you like to send it?
- How many stamps do you need?
- Would you like to purchase insurance for the package?

★ A: This package is very fragile.
  B: _____?

★ A: I want to buy some stamps, please.
  B: _____?

★ A: I'd like to send this to Canada.
  B: _____?

5. Role Plays

Look at the situations and act out the role plays with your partner.

Role A

You need to mail a package. Your package must arrive in Australia in three days or less, but you only have $50.00 with you. Get a price and send the package the fastest way possible.

1. Say where you want to send the item.
2. Explain when it needs to be delivered.
3. Tell the postal worker how you would like to mail it.

Role B

You work in the post office. A customer asks to mail a package to Australia. Overnight delivery for an item of that weight is $75 and three-day is $49.

1. Ask when the customer needs the item delivered by.
2. Ask to weigh the item and give the customer a price.
3. Ask for the customer's decision on how to ship the item.

Situation #1

Role A

You are an employee at a post office. A customer comes in to change his or her mailing address.

1. Ask the customer what he or she needs to do.
2. Have the customer confirm his or her current address.
3. Ask the customer to give his or her new address.

Role B

You need to change your mailing address. Go to the post office and ask for help from a postal worker.

1. Say what you need to do.
2. State your current address.
3. Tell your new address.

Situation #2

Situational Collocations!

Look at the collocations and try making your own sentences.

postal code	Postal code must contain only numbers.
fill out form	You need to fill out this form if it's worth over $10,000.
business days	The delivery typically occurs in 2 or 3 business days.
air freight	Our company usually sends goods by air freight.
return shipment	Dry ice is not allowed with the return shipment feature.
poor condition	The parcel arrived in poor condition.
shipping address	If necessary, please update your shipping address below.
make adjustment	Can I make an adjustment to my order?

1.
2.

The Post Office

Postal Services Facts

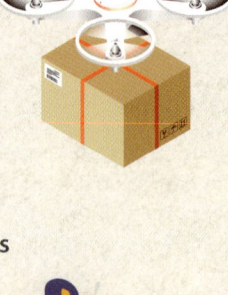

From 1917-1920, people could 'post' children as a parcel in the USA. This was later banned in July 13, 1920.

In 2001, the German post office started teaching dog psychology to its postmen.

Just during 2017-2018 in the UK, postmen were attacked by dogs 2,275 times. This is 8% less than 2016.

In 2017, FedEx delivered an endangered species, the Giant Panda, from Washington to China.

Amazon and UPS are working on new innovative delivery methods using drones.

6. Cultural Discussion Questions

Talk about the questions in as much detail as possible.

1. What kinds of things can you do at a post office in your country?
2. How has the post office changed over the last 10 years in your country?
3. How much does it cost to mail a letter in your country? How much has the price risen since you were young?
4. Is mail still delivered to your door in your country?

Did You Know?

Read and discuss how you feel about each fact.

1. Did you know the **US Postal Service** is the US's **largest domestic retail network**? It's bigger than McDonald's, Starbucks and Wal-Mart combined.

2. Did you know that December 20th is the busiest mailing day of the year in North America? On that day, an average of **801 million** letters, cards, and packages are processed each year.

Packing Materials

When you wrap up an item to mail, you can use a variety of materials to pack the item. Here are the four main materials people use to keep their packages safe during shipping. Guess what the name of each is and discuss when you might use it.

Answer: (1) packing peanuts (2) Packing Rope (3) Corrugated Cardboard/Fiberboards (4) Bubble Wrap

7. Slang & Idioms

Match the slang phrases and idioms with their definitions and use them to complete the sentences below.

1. ___ care package
2. ___ junk mail
3. ___ dead mail
4. ___ lost in the mail
5. ___ snail mail

A. sent by mail but never delivered to the person addressed to
B. mail that cannot be delivered to the addressee or returned to the sender
C. the ordinary postal system as opposed to email
D. unwanted or unsolicited advertising or promotional material received through the mail
E. a parcel of food, money, or luxury items sent to a loved one who is away

1. Jenny sent out her wedding invitations by _____.
2. I didn't receive your letter. It must have been _____.
3. My mailbox was filled with nothing but _____.
4. The letter with no return address went back to the post office as _____.
5. I sent my sister a _____ while she was studying abroad to let her know I was thinking of her.

Wrapping Up!
Write down four things you learned from this lesson and review.

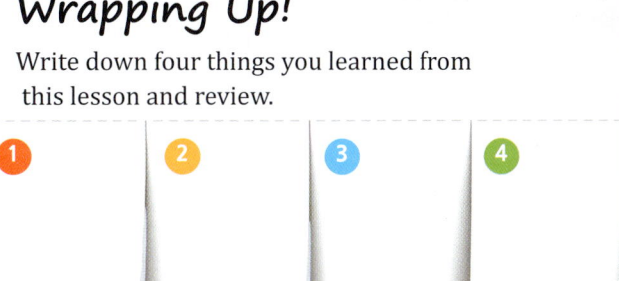

12 Picking Up a Prescription

» Learning Objective

Upon completion of this lesson, you will be able to...

speak with a pharmacist about a prescription.

» Expression Check

- ☑ I need this prescription filled, please.
- ☑ When do you think I can pick it up?
- ☑ Do you have health insurance?

1. Warm Up Activity

Describe what is happening in the picture.

Talk about the questions.

1. Where do you usually go to fill a prescription?
2. Which do you prefer - traditional or modern medicine?
3. Have you ever refilled a prescription that you finished?

2. Useful Expressions

Match the expressions (a-d) to its similar meaning (1-4).

A I need this prescription filled, please.

B When do you think I can pick it up?

C Take this three times a day at mealtimes.

D Do you have any allergies?

1 Swallow one pill at the same time as you eat your meals, three times a day.

2 Are you allergic to anything?

3 The doctor sent me here to get some medicine.

4 When can I return to get my medicine?

3. Key Conversation

Think of the useful expressions and practice the dialogue.

Will They Be Ready by Then?

Rebecca	I need to have this prescription filled, please.
Chris	Certainly, no problem.
Rebecca	When do you think I can pick it up?
Chris	It should be ready by this afternoon.
Rebecca	OK, thank you. Oh, and do you know how much this is going to cost me?
Chris	That depends. Do you have medical insurance?
Rebecca	I do have a plan through my company. I think it's with Home Plan.
Chris	OK, with Home Plan insurance, 70% of the cost will be covered, so these meds should only cost you $17.50 after deductions.
Rebecca	OK, that should be fine. I'll be back around 1:00 then to pick them up. Will they be ready by then?
Chris	Your prescription should be ready by then.

Questions

1. Do you think Rebecca comes to this pharmacy regularly?
2. Do you think Rebecca has a good health insurance plan?
3. When do you think Rebecca will return to pick up her medication?
4. Do you think the prescription will be ready when she returns?

Picking Up a Prescription

Can You Read This?

Have you ever received a hand-written note that you really could not read?

Today, many documents are written on computers, but did you know that in many places, prescriptions are still handwritten by doctors?

Doctors are famous for having bad handwriting. Many blame this on the number of notes and prescriptions that they need to quickly write.

Suppose you are traveling and suddenly become ill. You might visit a local hospital for a prescription from a doctor. When you take the prescription to the pharmacy, the pharmacist might have trouble making out some words and they will have to call the clinic to confirm. It might take a little longer, but you will get your prescription eventually.

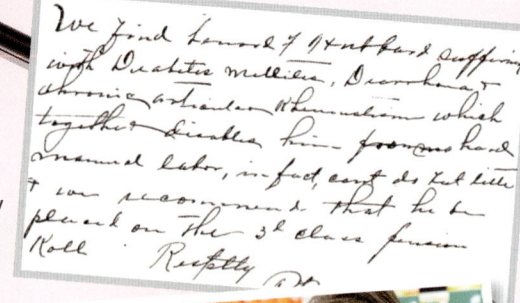

4. Language Practice

Using the key words, complete the sentences then practice making your own sentences.

Practice #1 — Taking medication

- take one / per day
- apply / ointment
- take / on an empty stomach

★ _____ this medicine _____.

★ _____ the _____ directly to the rash.

★ _____ tablet _____.

Practice #2 — Getting medicine

- prescription / filled
- time / pick up
- use / cream

★ What _____ can I _____ my prescription?

★ Can I get my _____ _____, please?

★ How should I _____ this _____?

Practice #3 — At the drug store

- Do you have health insurance?
- Are you allergic to anything?
- When will you pick up your prescription?

★ A: _____?
B: Yes, I'm allergic to penicillin.

★ A: _____?
B: Yes, I have a plan with Home Life.

★ A: _____?
B: I'll be back in half an hour.

Lesson 12 / Picking Up a Prescription

5. Role Plays

Look at the situations and act out the role plays with your partner.

Situation #1

Role A

You are a customer at a pharmacy. Get a prescription filled for medicine using your medical insurance.

1. Explain why you came to the pharmacy.
2. Check how much the medicine will cost.
3. Ask when you should return.

Role B

You are a pharmacist. Help your customer fill a prescription. The cost will be $15 with insurance and it will be ready in an hour.

1. Ask to see the prescription.
2. Ask the customer if he or she has insurance.
3. Tell the customer the cost and when the medicine will be ready.

Situation #2

Role A

You are a customer at a pharmacy. You are picking up a prescription that you dropped off earlier. Find out how to use the medicine that the pharmacist gives you.

1. Ask if the medicine is ready.
2. Ask how to use the medication.
3. Thank the pharmacist for his or her help.

Role B

A customer is picking up medicine for a rash. The ointment needs to be applied twice a day (in the morning and at night) and the customer needs to take one pill 30 minutes before each meal.

1. Say the prescription is ready.
2. Explain how to use the medication.
3. Confirm that the customer knows what to do.

Situational Collocations!

Look at the collocations and try making your own sentences.

feel nauseous	The antibiotics are making me feel nauseous.
knock out	My cold medication knocks me out.
on medication	Don't offer Jenny a drink – she is on medication.
on an empty stomach	Painkillers can be taken on an empty stomach.
side effect	Some medications have uncomfortable side effects, such as burping.
homemade remedy	My mom prefers homemade remedies to treat colds and mild illnesses.
over-the-counter	I bought some over-the-counter medicine to treat my stomach pain.
taken with/after food	Should these pills be taken with food?

1.
2.

Picking Up a Prescription

Natural Cold and Flu Remedies

It is no wonder that natural cold and flu remedies are popular – modern medicine has yet to offer a cure for these age-old ailments. See which cold and flu remedies show the most promise.

Vitamin C – A medical study has shown that people who work in cold weather and take Vitamin C are 50% less likely to get a cold than those who do not.

Chicken Soup – Inhaling the steam can ease nasal congestion. Sipping spoonfuls of fluid can help avoid dehydration.

Garlic – Garlic has long been touted for legendary germ-fighting abilities. One study showed garlic supplements may help prevent colds when taken daily.

Saltwater Gargle – For a sore throat, gargling with salt water can offer some relief.

Hot Tea – Inhaling the steam relieves congestion, while swallowing the fluid soothes the throat and keeps you hydrated.

Steam/Humidifier – Breathing in steam can break up congestion in the nasal passages, offering relief from a stuffy or runny nose.

6. Cultural Discussion Questions

Talk about the questions in as much detail as possible.

1. Are many drugs available over-the-counter in your country? What products can you buy directly from a pharmacist?
2. Describe the procedure for getting a prescription filled in your country.
3. Is it expensive to get prescription medicine in your country? What percentage does your insurance cover?
4. Do you feel like medical treatment is affordable in your country? Why or why not?

Did You Know?

Read and discuss how you feel about each fact.

1. Did you know that the *global pharmaceuticals market* is worth *$300 billion*?
2. Did you know that *Coca-Cola* was *invented by a pharmacist* named John Pemberton?

Going to See a Doctor vs Taking Over-the-Counter Medicine

When you are sick because of the problems below, where do you go? Do you go to see a doctor or to a drug store/pharmacy? Fill in the blanks below. "When I catch a cold, I usually go to a drugstore and buy over-the-counter medicine."

Cold or influenza	Drugstore
Diarrhea	
Digestive problems	
Headaches	
Heart problems	
Leg problems	
Rash	
Sinusitis	
Vomiting	
Sore muscles	
Minor burns and scalds	
Insomnia	

Over-the-Counter Medications

Prescription drugs normally require a doctor's order before they can be purchased at a pharmacy. These drugs are usually very potent, may be addictive if not used properly, and may have numerous adverse side effects. Over-the-counter drugs, however, do not need a doctor's order to be purchased. It is helpful to know that over-the-counter medication comes in a variety of packages and forms. Look at the examples below.

- Antacid tablets
- Allergy pills
- Cough drop lozenges
- Cold capsules
- Tube of muscle relaxant ointment
- Bottle of cough syrup

7. Slang & Idioms

Match the slang phrases and idioms with their definitions and use them to complete the sentences below.

1. ___ as right as rain
2. ___ back on his feet
3. ___ run down
4. ___ something going around
5. ___ horse pills

A. to be tired and somewhat unwell
B. a pill or tablet that is unusually or unreasonably large
C. contagious
D. to be perfectly fit and well
E. to be well again after being ill

1. There must be _____. You're the fourth person to tell me you are sick today!

2. A few more days of medicine and you'll be _____.

3. The doctor gave me these _____ for my cold; just looking at them makes my throat hurt!

4. I went to the doctor because lately, I've been feeling tired and _____.

5. Jim went to the doctor and he's hoping he'll be _____ by next week.

Wrapping Up!

Write down four things you learned from this lesson and review.

1.
2.
3.
4.

New Get Up To Speed+ Book 4
SLANG & IDIOM GLOSSARY

Lesson 1

drop me a line	to send someone a note or letter in a casual manner
hit us up	to contact someone
sent her a DM	to send a user a private message on a social media platform
shoot me an email	to send an email
touch base with	to communicate with someone, especially someone you haven't spoken with recently

Lesson 2

charged it	to pay with a credit card
hard cash	money in the form of coins or notes
money to burn	to have a lot of money to spend on things that are unnecessary
service charge	an extra charge added for a service
strapped	to be short of money

Lesson 3

burning a hole in my pocket	money that one wishes to spend quickly (often on something frivolous)
declare your purchase	to formally list items purchased abroad on a customs form
feel like a million bucks	to feel wonderful
making money hand over fist	to earn money fast and in large amounts
splurge	something that cost more money than one might ordinarily spend

Lesson 4

chow down	to eat food quickly or in an enthusiastic way
go back for seconds	to take a second helping of food
help yourself	to take some of what you want
leftovers	food that remains after some has been consumed
piece of cake	something easily achieved

Lesson 5

big name	a person who is famous in a certain sphere
face value	the value printed or depicted on a coin, banknote, postage stamp, or ticket
front row center	in or at the forefront of activity
scalper	a person who resells tickets for a large or quick profit
the pit	an area where the audience stands at the front of the stage

Lesson 6

baby bump	the protruding stomach of a woman who is visibly pregnant
baby shower	a gift-giving party to celebrate the delivery or expected birth of a child
bundle of joy	a newborn baby
sleep like a baby	to sleep soundly
with child	pregnant

Lesson 7

Actions speak louder than words	what you do shows your intentions more than what you say
for a good cause	to be worth doing or giving to because it will help other people
nonprofit	an organization not making or conducted primarily to make a profit
pay it forward	to respond to a person's kindness by being kind to someone else
take the credit	to allow people to believe that one did something that deserves praise

Lesson 8

bouncing off the walls	to be full of nervous excitement or agitation
chomping at the bit	to be very excited and anxious about an upcoming event
fired up	to be overwhelmingly excited
just around the corner	very close in time or distance
watching the clock	to keep looking at what the time is, usually because you are eager to leave

Lesson 9

buzzkill	a person or thing that has a depressing effect
hungover	suffering from a hangover after drinking alcohol
last call	closing time is approaching and any further drinks should be purchased immediately
on the house	a drink or meal in a bar or restaurant at the management's expense; free
wasted	under the influence of alcohol

Lesson 10

break the bank	to not have money because something cost too much
flat broke	to have no money
house poor	spending a large proportion of one's total income on home ownership
two pennies to rub together	to be extremely poor; to have very little money to spend
up to my ears	to have more of something than you can manage

Lesson 11

care package	a parcel of food, money, or luxury items sent to a loved one who is away
dead mail	mail that cannot be delivered to the addressee or returned to the sender
junk mail	unwanted or unsolicited advertising or promotional material received through the mail
lost in the mail	sent by mail but never delivered to the person addressed to
snail mail	the ordinary postal system as opposed to email

Lesson 12

as right as rain	to be perfectly fit and well
back on his feet	to be well again after being ill
horse pills	a pill or tablet that is unusually or unreasonably large
run down	to be tired and somewhat unwell
something going around	contagious

New Get Up To Speed+ Book 4
ANSWER KEY

Lesson 1

Useful Expressions

a 4
b 3
c 2
d 1

Language Practice

Practice #1
★ impatient / call me back
★ tired / voicemails
★ worried / reply to my texts

Practice #2
★ work
★ all
★ all

Practice #3
★ occupied with
★ busy getting ready for
★ get online

Slang & Idioms

1	C	shoot me an email
2	D	touch base with
3	A	drop me a line
4	B	sent her a DM
5	E	hit us up

Lesson 2

Useful Expressions

a 3
b 4
c 2
d 1

Language Practice

Practice #1
★ the bill
★ all
★ all

Practice #2
★ all
★ all
★ credit card

Practice #3
★ bring the bill
★ settle up
★ Just the check

Slang & Idioms

1	D	strapped
2	C	service charge
3	B	charged it
4	E	money to burn
5	A	hard cash

Lesson 3

Useful Expressions

a 2
b 1
c 3
d 4

Language Practice

Practice #1
★ engraved
★ total carat weight
★ platinum

Practice #2
★ under $1,000 or up to $500
★ $1,000 to $2,000
★ under $1,000 or up to $500

Practice #3

- ★ good exchange policy
- ★ certificate of authenticity
- ★ warranty

Slang & Idioms

1	B	burning a hole in my pocket
2	E	feel like a million bucks
3	D	splurge
4	C	making money hand over fist
5	A	declare your purchase

Lesson 4

Useful Expressions

a 3
b 4
c 1
d 2

Language Practice

Practice #1
- ★ hot dishes
- ★ short on
- ★ bringing salad

Practice #2
- ★ all
- ★ all
- ★ pasta salad

Practice #3
- ★ planning on / the potluck
- ★ food / to bring
- ★ people / coming to

Slang & Idioms

1	D	go back for seconds
2	E	piece of cake
3	B	help yourself
4	C	leftovers
5	A	chow down

Lesson 5

Useful Expressions

a 3
b 2
c 1
d 4

Language Practice

Practice #1
- ★ 9:00 show / Saturday or piano concert / May 12th
- ★ 9:00 show / Saturday or piano concert / May 12th
- ★ musical / weekend

Practice #2
- ★ four general admission
- ★ two / in the center
- ★ three seats / orchestra pit

Practice #3
- ★ cheaper / box office
- ★ more convenient / online
- ★ fast / ticketing machine

Slang & Idioms

1	C	the pit
2	B	front row center
3	D	scalper
4	E	face value
5	A	big name

Lesson 6

Useful Expressions

a 3
b 4
c 2
d 1

New Get Up To Speed+ Book 4
ANSWER KEY

Language Practice

Practice #1
★ She looks so much like you!
★ He's as cute as a button.
★ How are mother and baby doing?

Practice #2
★ sleeping through
★ mother's eyes
★ adorable face

Practice #3
★ When do you get to take her home?
★ How old is the baby now?
★ When will you bring him in for us to meet?

Slang & Idioms

1	D	sleep like a baby
2	A	baby shower
3	E	baby bump
4	C	bundle of joy
5	B	with child

Lesson 7

Useful Expressions
a 3
b 1
c 4
d 2

Language Practice

Practice #1
★ homeless shelter
★ soup kitchen
★ food bank

Practice #2
★ elderly / hospice or dogs / animal shelter
★ elderly / hospice or dogs / animal shelter
★ garbage / park

Practice #3
★ information
★ take place
★ Who will benefit from

Slang & Idioms

1	B	nonprofit
2	E	take the credit
3	D	for a good cause
4	C	Actions speak louder than words
5	A	pay it forward

Lesson 8

Useful Expressions
a 3
b 4
c 1
d 2

Language Practice

Practice #1
★ all
★ this weekend or after work on Friday
★ this weekend or after work on Friday

Practice #2
★ all
★ all
★ get away from it all or knock off early

Practice #3
★ can't wait
★ counting down the minutes
★ relax and take it easy

Slang & Idioms

| 1 | A | just around the corner |
| 2 | D | fired up |

3	B	chomping at the bit
4	E	watching the clock
5	C	bouncing off the walls

Lesson 9

Useful Expressions

a 4
b 1
c 3
d 2

Language Practice

Practice #1
★ another round
★ drop by
★ grab a drink

Practice #2
★ whatever's on tap
★ promotion
★ after work

Practice #3
★ at / in
★ come along
★ Stop by

Slang & Idioms

1	B	buzzkill
2	D	last call
3	A	wasted
4	E	on the house
5	C	hungover

Lesson 10

Useful Expressions

a 3
b 1
c 4
d 2

Language Practice

Practice #1
★ interest rate
★ insurance
★ down payment

Practice #2
★ all
★ all
★ all

Practice #3
★ went broke
★ credit score
★ debt

Slang & Idioms

1	E	break the bank
2	C	house poor
3	D	up to my ears
4	A	flat broke
5	B	two pennies to rub together

Lesson 11

Useful Expressions

a 3
b 4
c 1
d 2

Language Practice

Practice #1
★ letter / airmail or package / priority mail
★ a sheet of / stamps
★ letter / airmail or package / priority mail

New Get Up To Speed+ Book 4
ANSWER KEY

Practice #2
★ letter / airmail or document / priority mail
★ letter / airmail or document / priority mail
★ package / the US

Practice #3
★ Would you like to purchase insurance for the package?
★ How many stamps do you need?
★ How would you like to send it?

Slang & Idioms

1	E	snail mail
2	D	lost in the mail
3	B	junk mail
4	A	dead mail
5	C	care package

Lesson 12

Useful Expressions

a	3
b	4
c	1
d	2

Language Practice

Practice #1
★ Take / on an empty stomach
★ Apply / ointment
★ Take one / per day

Practice #2
★ time / pick up
★ prescription / filled
★ use / cream

Practice #3
★ Are you allergic to anything?
★ Do you have health insurance?
★ When will you pick up your prescription?

Slang & Idioms

1	D	something going around
2	E	as right as rain
3	A	horse pills
4	C	run down
5	B	back on his feet